Microsoft System Center Configuration Manager Advanced Deployment

Design, implement, and configure System Center Configuration Manager 2012 R2 with the help of real-world examples

Martyn Coupland

professional expertise distilled

BIRMINGHAM - MUMBAI

Microsoft System Center Configuration Manager Advanced Deployment

First published: September 2014

Production reference: 1180914

Published by Packt Publishing Ltd.
Livery Place
35 Livery Street
Birmingham B3 2PB, UK.

ISBN 978-1-78217-208-6

www.packtpub.com

Cover image by Suyog Gharat (yogiee@me.com)

Credits

Author
Martyn Coupland

Reviewers
Steve Barnard
Brian Mason
Torsten Meringer
Greg Ramsey

Commissioning Editor
James Jones

Acquisition Editor
James Jones

Content Development Editor
Susmita Panda Sabat

Technical Editors
Shashank Desai
Sebastian Rodrigues

Copy Editors
Insiya Morbiwala
Laxmi Subramanian
Stuti Srivastava

Project Coordinator
Neha Thakur

Proofreaders
Simran Bhogal
Maria Gould
Ameesha Green

Indexer
Tejal Soni

Graphics
Ronak Dhruv
Disha Haria

Production Coordinator
Nilesh R. Mohite

Cover Work
Nilesh R. Mohite

About the Author

Martyn Coupland is a senior consultant at Inframon, which is a UK System Center consultancy company. He specializes in client and cloud technologies, but he also has knowledge of the whole System Center suite and spends time with customers, helping them design and implement System Center solutions.

He has a background in support, and his career, like many others, started on the service desk in IT, performing first line support. Apart from his experience with System Center, Martyn also has experience in programming languages such as C# and web programming languages such as PHP, HTML, CSS, and JavaScript.

Acknowledgments

The past few years have been an incredible journey. The opportunity to write this book is just part of that journey, and I have so many people to thank for this.

My immediate thanks go to James and the rest of the staff at Packt Publishing for making this possible; the whole team has been great over the past few months. Secondly, I would like to thank Gordon and Sean at Inframon for believing in my ability and making my job the best journey ever. It is safe to say that without their belief, trust, and faith, my life would have been very different today.

Another thank you must go to my previous manager, Sarah, who also helped my career in a huge way. She is a dedicated person who always puts her team before her, and for this, I am grateful. She remains a friend today, so here's thanking her in a way I never thought I would be able to.

My final two thanks are the biggest. The first one goes out to my parents for always believing in me, trusting my career choices, and helping me through life; I couldn't have asked for two better people to help bring me up.

Finally, I would like to thank my wife, Kirsty, who is my best friend, the person I turn to for help, and the person I trust the most and love. Consulting is hard work not just for me but for Kirsty as well. I spend most weeks away from home with only the comfort of her voice during the week; it makes weekends so special. She has stuck with me throughout my incredible journey over the past two years; I couldn't have done it without her in so many ways. So, Kirsty, this is my way of saying thank you for trusting me, and thank you for sticking with me through the many good times we have had as well as the tough and difficult times.

About the Reviewers

Steve Barnard is a System Center consultant and has been involved in the IT industry for 15 years after starting out as an accountant. After making a career change, he started out in the field of desktop support for a large educational establishment before moving on to server administration along with desktop deployment. This involved working with Server 2003 and early versions of MDT and BDD. He started working with Configuration Manager during the later releases of SMS 2003 and has been involved with the product ever since. He currently works at Inframon Ltd., which is a System Center consultancy company, designing and configuring System Center solutions for medium- and large-scale organizations.

Brian Mason is a systems engineer at Wells Fargo, where he manages over 350,000 resources with CM. Brian is a Microsoft MVP for Configuration Manager (CM). He currently runs the Minnesota System Center User Group and its website, where he blogs as well. He has also worked on *Microsoft System Center 2012 Configuration Manager: Administration Cookbook, Packt Publishing*.

Torsten Meringer, ConfigMgr MVP since 2005, is a self-employed senior consultant who is located in Germany. He started his own business in 1999 and primarily focuses on designing, migrating, deploying, training, automating, and troubleshooting Microsoft's deployment and management solutions such as System Center Configuration Manager, System Center Orchestrator, and Microsoft Deployment Toolkit in small- to large-scale companies that have a range of 500 to more than 200,000 clients. He manages the German ConfigMgr blog, http://www.mssccmfaq.de, and holds various MCT, MCSA, MCSE, MCTS, and MCITP:EA certifications. He is also an author and a speaker at various Microsoft events.

Greg Ramsey, Enterprise and Client Management MVP, holds the position of Enterprise Tools Strategist at Dell, Inc. He has a BS degree in Computer Sciences and Engineering from Ohio State University. Greg co-authored *System Center Configuration Manager 2007 Unleashed, System Center 2012 R2 Configuration Manager Unleashed, Sams Publishing,* and *Microsoft System Center 2012 Configuration Manager: Administration Cookbook, Packt Publishing.* He is a co-founder of the Ohio SMS Users Group and the Central Texas Systems Management User Group.

www.PacktPub.com

Support files, eBooks, discount offers, and more

You might want to visit www.PacktPub.com for support files and downloads related to your book.

Did you know that Packt offers eBook versions of every book published, with PDF and ePub files available? You can upgrade to the eBook version at www.PacktPub.com and as a print book customer, you are entitled to a discount on the eBook copy. Get in touch with us at service@packtpub.com for more details.

At www.PacktPub.com, you can also read a collection of free technical articles, sign up for a range of free newsletters and receive exclusive discounts and offers on Packt books and eBooks.

http://PacktLib.PacktPub.com

Do you need instant solutions to your IT questions? PacktLib is Packt's online digital book library. Here, you can access, read and search across Packt's entire library of books.

Why subscribe?

- Fully searchable across every book published by Packt
- Copy and paste, print and bookmark content
- On demand and accessible via web browser

Free access for Packt account holders

If you have an account with Packt at www.PacktPub.com, you can use this to access PacktLib today and view nine entirely free books. Simply use your login credentials for immediate access.

Instant updates on new Packt books

Get notified! Find out when new books are published by following @PacktEnterprise on Twitter, or the *Packt Enterprise* Facebook page.

Table of Contents

Preface

In this book, we will go further into Configuration Manager compared to the other books you may have read. While many books on this subject focus on the fundamentals or act as an introduction, this book is aimed at readers with a solid knowledge of Configuration Manager already and who are looking to enhance their skills or see some real-world examples of how it can be used.

Before we get into too much detail, I would like to begin with a brief introduction to Configuration Manager so we are all on the same page. Configuration Manager has long been known for its ability to distribute software; this is the primary reason for the use of Configuration Manager. However, Configuration Manager also contains many other abilities, such as the ability to perform one-off or mass deployments of operating systems, manage your security updates, meter software usage on clients, collect valuable inventory information, and perform powerful reporting, to name a few.

What this book covers

Chapter 1, Designing Complex Hierarchies, explores how to design complex hierarchies. As the book is aimed at more advanced users, it is likely they will be exposed to larger hierarchies. You will learn how to get the best from your design and create a high-quality environment. We will discuss why we make design decisions and discuss the alternatives.

Chapter 2, Implementing Security with Certificates, explains the concepts behind adding security to your environment using certificates to secure communication in your site.

Chapter 3, Working with Inventory, Asset Intelligence, and Software Metering, helps you gain an understanding of how to use both software and hardware inventory to gain valuable information about your environment. You will then discover how to use this knowledge to be able to remove unused software automatically.

Chapter 4, *Security with Endpoint Protection*, explores how to deploy System Center Endpoint Protection to help protect your clients and manage the policies around the product. You'll also learn how to update endpoint protection with the latest definition updates.

Chapter 5, *Advanced Content Management*, explains how Configuration Manager manages content and how to use distribution points in certain deployment scenarios. You will also gain an understanding of how to use cloud-based distribution points as well as understand the flow of content within Configuration Manager.

Chapter 6, *Application Deployment*, explores the concepts involved with setting up and deploying applications in Configuration Manager. This includes setting up dependencies and requirements and exploring the deployment options available.

Chapter 7, *Deploying Windows 8.1 and Windows Server 2012 R2*, explores the concepts to deploy Windows 8.1 and Windows Server 2012 R2. We will walk through two real-world examples with sample scripts, where required, to create a usable Windows deployment for both the client and server.

Chapter 8, *Deploying Security Updates*, explains how to secure your environment by deploying Microsoft security updates to your clients.

Chapter 9, *Advanced Reporting*, explains how to create custom reports as well as how to use Report Builder with SQL Server Reporting Services. You will learn how to deploy reports and create functional charts that show live data from their site.

Chapter 10, *Preventing Configuration Drift*, explains the importance of monitoring your environment for configuration drift and how we can resolve this problem.

Chapter 11, *Managing Bring Your Own Device and Mobility*, explains how to use your Configuration Manager environment to address management issues that have arisen due to the rise in personal device usage in the office.

Chapter 12, *Advanced Troubleshooting*, focuses on troubleshooting all the concepts described in each chapter. You will understand where to look for errors, which logfiles are important for different functions, and how to use toolkit items to troubleshoot problems.

What you need for this book

For this book, the following software is required:

- Operating systems:
    - ° Server: Windows Server 2012 R2
    - ° Client: Windows 7 SP1 or higher

- Software:
    - ° Microsoft SQL Server 2012 SP2
    - ° Microsoft System Center 2012 Configuration Manager R2

- Platform:
    - ° Active Directory

Note that all the preceding software, while proprietary, can be downloaded in a trial edition that will entitle you to 180 days of usage without the need for a full license key.

Who this book is for

In order to get the most out of the book, it is recommended that you have the following experience:

- Knowledge of systems management with Configuration Manager
- Knowledge about managing servers
- Basic knowledge of SQL Server and SQL Reporting Services
- Solid, all-round IT knowledge

Conventions

In this book, you will find a number of styles of text that distinguish between different kinds of information. Here are some examples of these styles, and an explanation of their meaning.

Code words in text, database table names, folder names, filenames, file extensions, pathnames, dummy URLs, user input, and Twitter handles are shown as follows: "Once the manual schedule has completed, check the `MP_Hinv.log` and `dataldr.log` files on the server."

A block of code is set as follows:

```
Echo Adding Trusted Root Certificate
certutil -addstore -f "ROOT" "%~dp0MyTrustedRoot.cer"
echo Import Client Certificate
```

Any command-line input or output is written as follows:

```
Import-Module ServerManager
```

New terms and **important words** are shown in bold. Words that you see on the screen, in menus or dialog boxes for example, appear in the text like this: "Right-click on your site and then select **Properties**."

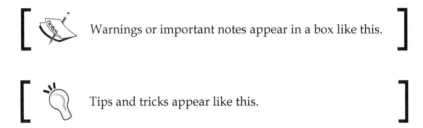

Warnings or important notes appear in a box like this.

Tips and tricks appear like this.

Reader feedback

Feedback from our readers is always welcome. Let us know what you think about this book—what you liked or may have disliked. Reader feedback is important for us to develop titles that you really get the most out of.

To send us general feedback, simply send an e-mail to feedback@packtpub.com, and mention the book title via the subject of your message.

If there is a topic that you have expertise in and you are interested in either writing or contributing to a book, see our author guide on www.packtpub.com/authors.

Customer support

Now that you are the proud owner of a Packt book, we have a number of things to help you to get the most from your purchase.

Downloading the example code

You can download the example code files for all Packt books you have purchased from your account at `http://www.packtpub.com`. If you purchased this book elsewhere, you can visit `http://www.packtpub.com/support` and register to have the files e-mailed directly to you.

Errata

Although we have taken every care to ensure the accuracy of our content, mistakes do happen. If you find a mistake in one of our books—maybe a mistake in the text or the code—we would be grateful if you would report this to us. By doing so, you can save other readers from frustration and help us improve subsequent versions of this book. If you find any errata, please report them by visiting `http://www.packtpub.com/submit-errata`, selecting your book, clicking on the **errata submission form** link, and entering the details of your errata. Once your errata are verified, your submission will be accepted and the errata will be uploaded on our website, or added to any list of existing errata, under the Errata section of that title. Any existing errata can be viewed by selecting your title from `http://www.packtpub.com/support`.

Piracy

Piracy of copyright material on the Internet is an ongoing problem across all media. At Packt, we take the protection of our copyright and licenses very seriously. If you come across any illegal copies of our works, in any form, on the Internet, please provide us with the location address or website name immediately so that we can pursue a remedy.

Please contact us at `copyright@packtpub.com` with a link to the suspected pirated material.

We appreciate your help in protecting our authors, and our ability to bring you valuable content.

Questions

You can contact us at `questions@packtpub.com` if you are having a problem with any aspect of the book, and we will do our best to address it.

1
Designing Complex Hierarchies

The essential component to a well-performing hierarchy is a good design. Without a good design, you can find yourself having issues in your environment, such as under- or over-utilized resources or an environment that does not meet the initial requirements. The design should be a single point where everyone can look and see how the hierarchy should be built, operated, and maintained.

In this chapter, we will explore many components that make up a good design. We will be covering the following topics:

- How to make sure you select the appropriate site system server
- How to design fault tolerant environments
- How to properly back up and restore a Configuration Manager site
- How to design for multiple trusted forests
- How to design for nontrusted forests
- A working design scenario example

Selecting the appropriate site system server

As we already know, a Configuration Manager hierarchy starts with either a central administration site and a primary site in a hierarchy or just a single standalone primary site. Unlike in Configuration Manager 2012 RTM, in Configuration Manager 2012 SP1 you cannot add a central administration site later; you can do this in the R2 version. It should be noted though that you cannot remove a central administration site later on with any version of Configuration Manager 2012. This means you no longer have to make any large assumptions about the size of your hierarchy years down the line.

When to use a central administration site

It is important to mention at this point that the central administration site is not a direct replacement for the old central site in the previous versions. The way the hierarchy works is different from the previous versions, so it would be difficult to compare the two. In Configuration Manager 2012, the central administration site is used as a central location for both administration and reporting. While some site system roles can be deployed to the central administration site, you cannot assign clients to the central administration site.

In the previous versions of Configuration Manager, we used a central site to address many issues, such as:

- Splitting the management of servers and client machines
- Segregating permissions between sites
- Applying different client settings to servers and client machines
- Internal political reasons

Configuration Manager 2012 has gone a long way in answering many of these points, meaning that we can now deploy a single-flat hierarchy, which is both easy to manage and gives us the flexibility to delegate the management of different environments or devices to our support teams as well as properly define permissions for the whole hierarchy rather than at a single-site level.

 If you are coming away from a Configuration Manager 2007 environment, think about the reasons you may have had to deploy multiple sites in Configuration Manager 2012. Those reasons have probably gone.

Now, the golden rule for a central administration site is that if you are managing more than one primary site, then you require a central administration site to manage them both centrally. For this reason, most of you will not require a central administration site. This is because a standalone primary site can support up to 100,000 clients.

It should also be noted that the design should be as simple as the requirements allow and that a central administration does not provide high availability, which is a common misconception.

To give you an idea in terms of supported numbers of clients, when you are supporting Windows Server, Windows Client, and Windows Embedded operating systems as well as Linux and UNIX clients, then a standalone primary site will support up to 100,000 clients.

Devices that are managed by Windows Intune or the Exchange Server Connector will support up to 50,000 clients and finally, mobile devices enrolled by Configuration Manager, mobile device legacy clients, such as WinCE 5.0, WinCE 6.0, WinCE 7.0, and Windows Mobile 6.0 and Mac OS X clients can support 25,000 clients.

While it is important that you do not over specify the site, it is also important that the site is designed fit for this purpose. Try to move away from the design rules that were used in the previous versions of Configuration Manager; while those designs will still be valid, it may not be the correct way to do it anymore.

> Adding a central administration site brings extra complexities, such as the need for SQL replication and additional skills when it comes to troubleshooting the environment.

Determining the location of primary sites

In the largest hierarchies, it is not uncommon to see multiple primary sites. We have just seen how, technically, you don't need to deploy multiple primary site servers if you are not managing over 100,000 clients. Designing Configuration Manager in the most technically sound way every time will end up causing you potentially more problems than you would like.

> Always take into account the business requirements of your organization and make sure you understand the strategy your business is taking; this may mean that you have to break the best technical design.

Some common reasons for not deploying a technically sound solution would be as follows:

- Legal reasons
- Internal political reasons
- Regulatory reasons

From experience, it is not uncommon to have to put in multiple primary sites when one would have done the job. While it is always great to design a solution that does the job without spending lots of money, always remember that functionality and flexibility should come first; however, for legal and regulatory reasons, this may not be possible. If this is the case, make sure this is highlighted in the design.

If you know your company is flexible in the way they work, for example, offices that appear and disappear quickly, often with large numbers of employees and equipment that need to be managed, then make sure the hierarchy you design can accommodate this solution and is flexible enough to support those requirements. This example is a fairly common one in the construction industry where project offices pop up and pop down at a moment's notice.

In this scenario, the most technically sound design would mean you having to admit that your hierarchy cannot support these clients properly without some re-design; this is not a situation you want to be in.

Working with secondary sites

For a long time, secondary sites in Configuration Manager have been seen as a bit of a dark art. You shouldn't think of them like that. With the release of Configuration Manager 2012, it is not uncommon that you can just replace your existing secondary sites with distribution points.

The reason for this is that in Configuration Manager 2007, a secondary site would commonly be used because of the sender, which provided throttling, scheduling, and compression of the traffic, if required. However, these capabilities have been added to the distribution point in Configuration Manager 2012.

Secondary sites do still have their place though. In Configuration Manager 2012, secondary sites take part in replication just like the central administration site and the primary site. Portions of the database are not replicated down to the secondary site from the primary site; the replication that is used makes this a highly efficient process. By default, a secondary site installation will automatically deploy SQL Server Express unless you specify an installation of the SQL Server you have already deployed.

The replication that is used in Configuration Manager 2012 is not the native SQL Replication that we are used to. Instead the replication is taking advantage of the SQL Server Broker Service. The broker is a native SQL functionality, which supports messaging and queuing. This is known as the **Data Replication Service (DRS)**.

When you are looking at your network topology and deciding if you should place a secondary site at that location, ask yourself the following questions:

- Does this location have more than 500 clients and less than 5,000 clients?
- Do I need to compress the traffic going to the site?
- Do I need to control the flow of traffic flowing up the hierarchy?
- Do I need a local management point?
- Do I need a local Software Update Point?

If you can look at a specific location and answer any of those questions as yes, then you will probably need to deploy a secondary site. Let's dig into the preceding questions a little more; this should give us some pointers to help make our decision.

Client count

The number of clients you intend to support is a really important factor. The main reason is that the secondary site supports communication from up to 5,000 clients. If you have more than 5,000 clients at one location, then regardless of network connectivity, you will potentially want to look at putting a primary site here anyway rather than using a secondary site.

Another question for client count is to ask yourself if you want 500 clients getting policy over the network to a remote location? The content can be addressed with distribution points; what we are attempting to address in this scenario are too many clients communicating with a management point over the WAN.

 Information on the estimation of client network traffic can be found in a very useful TechNet article at `http://bit.ly/1sZTHfY`.

Traffic control

Do you have enough physical network bandwidth to support this amount of traffic? This is the question we are asking here. This will determine if we need to compress or control the flow of traffic that is heading up the hierarchy.

Regardless of the number of clients communicating, we do not want to saturate the network with the management traffic.

 When we say regardless of client numbers, quality of service on our network can go a long way in addressing these issues. So don't place a secondary site just for the sake of 30 clients, as this will end up giving you administrative headaches.

The local management point

Unlike the distribution point, we cannot control which management point the clients report to at a primary site, when we have multiple management points. For this reason, the only way we can control this is by using a secondary site. The same would go for the Software Update Point; this is another service of the hierarchy like the management point. We are unable to control which Software Update Point the client will use at any given time.

What should you do when you are unsure?

After applying the rules set out in the preceding section, we might still be unsure about whether or not we will need a secondary site. One of the great things about Configuration Manager is the simplicity and ease with which we can deploy and modify the hierarchy from within the console.

 You can always deploy a distribution point to the location in question; just monitor the link with your network team, and adjust the infrastructure if required.

Designing fault-tolerant hierarchies

In today's world, the systems we design and deploy are under more pressure than ever. We are expected to design systems with less money to implement, which can lead to design mistakes or errors in judgment. One area that usually suffers from this is the design of fault tolerance or disaster recovery. In a legacy world, Configuration Manager has been seen as a tool only used by IT departments to manage machines and has often given little business benefit. With the new wave of mobile devices, tablet devices, and other scenarios, such as bring your own device, Configuration Manager has suddenly become a critical application that is used to manage all these devices from one single pane of glass.

It is no secret that true fault tolerance in the form of clustering is something missing from Configuration Manager but that does not mean we still cannot produce a design that is able to switch to a disaster recovery scenario or provide a fault-tolerant service.

Fault tolerance in site systems

The central administration site, primary site, and the secondary site are all site systems. These themselves cannot be part of a cluster or any type of load balancing. What we can do though is make the database that stores our entire configuration, inventory, and other information highly available.

This can be done in a number of ways, for example, we can provide high availability using a traditional SQL cluster service. Both of these configurations allow us to make the database highly available.

Back to the site systems, if we are deploying our site system servers as virtual machines, then we can take advantage of replica in Hyper-V or similar technologies in VMware. This will make our site system server switch, should the workload need moving in the event of a failure. In this scenario, if you are deploying the site system server on the same server where SQL Server is deployed, then we might not need to worry about making the database highly available.

Fault tolerance in site-system roles

Any other service you deploy in Configuration Manager, such as the management point, distribution point, and fallback status point, to name a few, is known as a site system role. In some instances, we can create multiple instances of these roles to create tolerance but not in the sense of a cluster.

Some site system roles you can only deploy as one instance per hierarchy, for example, this is true of the Endpoint Protection Point where you can only deploy one instance of the role per hierarchy.

The management point is a good exception to this. While we cannot pick and choose which management point a client will communicate with in a primary site, we can deploy multiple management point servers to provide options to the client. If our hierarchy is running in an HTTPS configuration, then management points that are HTTPS enabled will be ordered above any HTTP management points by the client while it is selecting a management point to use.

The same can be said for the distribution point: we can deploy multiple instances of the distribution point to give the clients options when deciding which to use for downloading content. Software Update Points can be added to an NLB cluster, for example, which must be configured using PowerShell. However, they can also, with newer versions of Configuration Manager, have multiple instances in the same hierarchy without the need for an NLB cluster.

Depending on the requirements of the design and how important Configuration Manager is in terms of its role in the recovery of a data center is the driving factor for building fault tolerance at the site system role side of the picture.

Backup and recovery in Configuration Manager

As with fault tolerance, incorporating information for the backup and recovery of any Configuration Manager site is an important subject. It is vital that this is designed properly; should the worst happen and you need to recover the site at any point, then the planning work you have done at this stage will be invaluable in ensuring the successful recovery of the site in a timely fashion.

Configuration Manager provides two backup options; the first is the easier of the two to implement and makes use of the built-in maintenance task called the Site Backup task, which is responsible for creating a backup of the site. The backup can be run at the central administration site and the primary site but not at the secondary site or any site system roles. A third option is also possible, which is the only backup of SQL.

The backup engine follows the instructions defined in the backup control file (`<Install Directory>\Inboxes\Smsbkup.box\Smsbkup.ctl`). You can modify this file to control how the backup runs.

In addition to this service, if you run **System Center 2012 Data Protection Manager** (**DPM**), you can use it to back up Configuration Manager if you are running at least Service Pack 1. To enable this, create a new protection group in DPM for the site database server. When you are on the **Select Group Members** page of the wizard, select the **SMS Writer** service from the data source list and then select the site database as the member.

 Configuration Manager does not support backup for a SQL Server cluster using a named instance when using DPM. However, it does support this when using the default instance.

When you recover the site from a DPM backup, in the setup wizard of Configuration Manager, select the **Use a site database that has been manually recovered** option to use the backup from DPM.

Advanced backup options

It is best practice for any infrastructure service to keep multiple backups. Various reasons exist for this; however, I will not go into many details here. By using the default backup site server task in Configuration Manager, the first time a maintenance task runs, a snapshot is created. The next time the backup runs, another snapshot is taken and the previous snapshot is overwritten. As a result of how the backup maintenance task works, you only have the most recent backup and have no way of recovering an earlier snapshot.

Thankfully, you can use a batch file, `AfterBackup.bat`, which is automatically run following the completion of the maintenance task. You must manually create this file if you need it at `<Install Directory>\Inboxes\Smsbkup.box`. If this file exists, then it will be automatically executed.

The file is a regular batch script so you can perform any actions you wish here. You can verify the completion of the maintenance task, which includes the execution of `AfterBackup.bat` from the **Component Status** node in the **Monitoring** workspace. Look for the `SMS_SITE_BACKUP` component and you should see a status message with an ID of 5040.

 To archive the backup snapshot, use a copy tool to move the backup to the appropriate location. You can then use your current enterprise backup solution to move the backup to a traditional tape, for example, using Robocopy (`Robocopy.exe Z:\Backup \\Server\Share\Backup /MIR`).

Additional backup tasks

While the backup maintenance task takes care of much of the site information and the database, it does not take care of everything. One example of this is that any custom reports that you create needs to be backed up manually.

The same is true for content files, which are part of applications and packages. The content library needs to be restored before you can redistribute any content to the distribution points. When the distribution manager starts to distribute content, it is copied from the site server to the distribution points. You must ensure that your backup solution includes both the content library and the package and application source locations for the site server.

Custom software updates that may have been published using **System Center Update Publisher 2011** (**SCUP**) must also be backed up. These are also not included as part of the backup maintenance task. SCUP uses a database to store the repository so it is also important to make sure this database is included in your backup plans. It should be noted that the database file for SCUP is located in each user's profile.

Finally, the user state migration data is also not included. This is information that may be used during operating system deployment to back up and restore user state from one machine to another during either a refresh or a replace scenario. You must manually back up the folders that are specified in the **Folder details** section of the **General** tab in the **State Migration Point** properties.

Restoring a Configuration Manager site

Unlike the previous versions of Configuration Manager, you can no longer use the **Recover a site** option from the **Start** menu on the site server. You can only start the recovery wizard from the installation media. The wizard is available in the regular setup.

 If your site was using database replicas on management points, before you can use them again, you must configure each replica. This includes both the publications and the subscriptions.

Once the setup has begun, you have the following two options that are available for the recovery of the failed site:

- **Recover the site server using an existing backup**: This option should be used if you have a backup of the Configuration Manager site, which was created as part of the Backup Site Server maintenance task.

- **Reinstall the site server**: This option is used when you have no backup available. Use the same site code and site database name as when the initial setup was performed; you will have to configure your site again like a normal installation.

For the site database, the following options are available as part of the recovery:

- **Recover the site database using a backup set**: This option should be used when you have a valid backup created by the maintenance task.

- **Create a new database for this site**: This option should be used when you do not have a site database backup available.

- **Use a site database that has been manually recovered**: This option should be used when you have already recovered the site but the database has been backed up using another method. For example, you would use this option when restoring from a DPM or SQL backup.

 Since Configuration Manager 2012 R2, you can specify an alternative restore location during the restoration process.

Post recovery tasks to complete the recovery

After the site and the database have been recovered, any password for accounts that are set up in Configuration Manager will need their password re-entered. Thankfully, the accounts that require this action to be performed are listed on the **Finished** page of the setup wizard after the recovery is complete. This information is also saved to `C:\ConfigMgrPostRecoveryActions.html` on the recovered site server.

Any Windows Server hotfixes that have been applied to the server will also be listed on the **Finished** page of the setup wizard and also in the preceding referenced file.

Designing to support trusted forests

Configuration Manager supports the deployment of site servers, such as the primary site and the secondary site across different forests when two-way trust is established between the two forests.

When you want to support multiple forests and a two-way trust exists, Configuration Manager does not require any additional configuration provided any firewalls have the appropriate ports opened and name resolution works between the forests. By default, Configuration Manager, even in this scenario, will configure the database replication between the sites and also the intersite file replication.

If you do not require a site system in the other forest, then Configuration Manager also supports the placement of site system roles in these environments. It may be overkill to provide the services of a primary site in another forest. When this situation arises, use the same rules to determine if you place a distribution point or a secondary site out in that forest; just because it's a different forest, it doesn't change how you treat that environment.

Additionally, with Configuration Manager 2012 R2, you can add multiple network access accounts, which can help with the support of trusted forests.

When clients are not in the same forest as the site server, Configuration Manager supports the following scenarios:

- The two-way forest trust exists between the site server and the forest of the client

- The site system role is located in the same forest as the client

- The client is on a workgroup computer

Clients that are members of an Active Directory domain can use Active Directory for service location when the site is published to their Active Directory forest. You can also publish site information to untrusted forests. Additional forests can be specified in the console other than the forest where the site server is installed. This can be done from within the **Active Directory Forests** node in the **Administration** workspace. Any forests that you specify in this node will be picked up by the **Active Directory Forest Discovery Agent** if it is enabled.

Designing to support nontrusted forests

In addition to supporting communication from clients that are in trusted forests, Configuration Manager also supports communication from clients that are in an un-trusted forest from the site server.

Configuration Manager will support the installation of site system roles in another nontrusted forest with two exceptions. The first is the application catalog web service point and the other is the out of band service point. Both of these roles must be installed in the same forest as the site server.

When you are deploying a management point in an un-trusted forest, it is very important that you configure a connection account to enable the management point to obtain information from the database. Make sure the domain account has permission in the database. This is the same for the enrollment point as well. You must also ensure that you use an account that has administrative permissions on the target server in the target domain to complete the installation.

You cannot deploy site systems, such as the central administration site, primary site, and secondary site across un-trusted forest boundaries. Only site system roles can be deployed in un-trusted forest scenarios.

Designing a sample hierarchy

We are going to finish off this chapter by looking at a scenario, which is fairly common. This example will use some of the rules that we have seen throughout this chapter and put them into practice. We will also see how the working of Configuration Manager 2012 helps in addressing some business requirements and look at our design decisions throughout the process and wrap up with how the design brings business benefits.

Our customer is currently running Configuration Manager 2007 to manage around 25,500 clients over three physical locations. The current hierarchy consists of one central site and four child primary sites; the company's headquarters are located in London with offices in New York and Chicago.

After a meeting with a customer, they have provided the following information to us about their current deployment of Configuration Manager 2007:

Location	Site type	Details
London	Central site	19,500 clients, configuration is using the company standard settings
London	Child primary	500 clients used by finance where different agent settings are specified
New York	Child primary	4,000 desktop clients, using the company standard settings
New York	Child primary	500 servers, inventory, and remote control are disabled
Chicago	Child primary	1,000 clients using the company standard settings

Business requirements

With any design, it is vital to capture the key business requirements not just from the technical members of the project team, but also from people like Service Managers and the CIO who may be closer to the business than you are and can provide valuable insight into key decisions that may affect your design.

In our example, a number of requirements have been captured:

- Provide centralized management of the hierarchy from the London office even for regional IT departments
- Regional IT departments outside of London must only be able to see and manage clients in their specific locations

- Unless other requirements dictate, all clients should have a default client settings policy applied
- Any member of the HR team must have remote control disabled on their device at all times
- Servers in New York and London must have inventory collected every four days
- Bandwidth between London and New York must be controlled because the network link is slow
- The amount of infrastructure for managing the hierarchy must be reduced from what is currently used
- It has also been requested that where possible, licensing costs be cut down

Design assumptions and risks

As many of you will no doubt have experienced, it is not uncommon to have an uncompleted set of requirements, which often mean you need to make assumptions in your design. Often these can come back to bite you later down the line. It is always important to make sure that you note down these assumptions and make sure you discuss them with the relevant people.

Make sure they understand the implications of the assumption and what might happen if the assumption is incorrect. Once you know this information, write it into your design and ensure you get the relevant people to sign off the design to make sure they are happy with your decisions and that they accept the assumptions you have made.

The exact same can be said for risks, these are as if not more important than assumptions. It is not uncommon to have risks on your deployment based on another project. For example, a risk might be that you cannot start your deployment until a new virtualized environment is deployed. The risk is that the environment is not ready in time to start your Configuration Manager deployment.

For our design, we have made some assumptions; you can see these listed out:

- Client numbers are constantly changing as projects are started and finished in different continents
- English will be the only language that is deployed to client workstations and servers
- All systems will be virtualized rather than using physical servers
- London, New York, and Chicago all contain local administrators
- Software update integration is not required in this phase of the project

It is important to understand that as the company starts new projects, this can mean new temporary locations of anything up to 10,000 clients, so it is important we provide flexibility.

Planning the new hierarchy

One of the big changes from Configuration Manager 2007 to Configuration Manager 2012 is the ability to deploy settings policies on a per collection basis rather than in Configuration Manager 2007 when they applied on a per site basis. With the information we have collected, this is going to come in very handy when we look at the final design.

The ability to also define security in a more granular way using role-based administration to give people access to perform set actions and then scoping their access down to Security Scopes will help with some of the defined requirements.

Not every design decision is black and white; sometimes we can have multiple options available to us for our design, and we need to make sure we pick the right option and justify that decision in our documentation.

Our design is no different, we have multiple options and considerations we need to look at to make the right decision. The following table lays out some of the options available to us when we look at addressing some of the challenges that we are facing:

Challenges	Design options
Centrally administering the site in London	• Deploy one standalone primary site in London to centrally manage all clients
	• Deploy a primary site at each location and then a central administration site in London
Content between London and New York will consume more bandwidth than what is desired and must be controlled	• Deploy distribution points with bandwidth control enabled
	• Enable Windows BranchCache
Address the requirement to manage bandwidth for client information sent from New York	• Allow clients to transfer their data unmanaged
	• Deploy a secondary site or primary site in New York to manage the bandwidth
The company standard set of client settings must apply to all clients	• Deploy a default set of client settings and override where applicable

Directly addressing the stated requirements

Now that we have looked at some of the challenges we are facing, we need to make decisions on each of the requirements. This will start forming the basis of the design that we will prepare.

First of all, we need to decide on the top of the hierarchy. With the information we have been provided, a central administration site will be the best fit. This addresses the requirement that the site should be centrally managed from one location. We could also have provided a standalone primary site, which would have achieved the same result; however, this restricts our hierarchy in terms of what we place at sites lower down the hierarchy. This is because if we place a secondary site in New York, which would be the preferred technical solution, this means we cannot expand late. Remember that we might suddenly have to manage two more offices with 10,000 clients at each location. At this point, we don't need to pay much attention to the ability to segregate management of systems to regional departments, as no matter how we design the site, this functionality will be available.

Next is the ability to control traffic between London and New York. First of all, we need to deploy a single primary site as part of our hierarchy, which is also in London; this will be connected to our central administration site. This primary site will service the 20,000 clients that are located in London and combine down two existing sites, the old central site and child primary site. We cannot assign clients to the central administration site so we need a primary site in the hierarchy.

For New York, we will also place a primary site. This configuration has been chosen for the following reasons:

- Site-to-site configurations can address the bandwidth control requirements to transfer content from London

- Settings are managed centrally so we only need to deploy a single primary site, which is joined to the hierarchy

- As the link is slow, we do not want the 4,500 clients in New York sending their inventory and policy requests over the network to London

- Any future growth can be handled by implementing a primary site today rather than a secondary site or site system roles

Finally, in Chicago we deploy a secondary site that is hanging off the New York primary site. We do this because although the links between Chicago and New York are fast, this site has 1,000 clients. Additionally, from an administrative point of view, it makes logical sense to create the secondary site off the other site in North America, rather than creating it from the primary site in London.

The following diagram shows how the core of our hierarchy will look with this configuration:

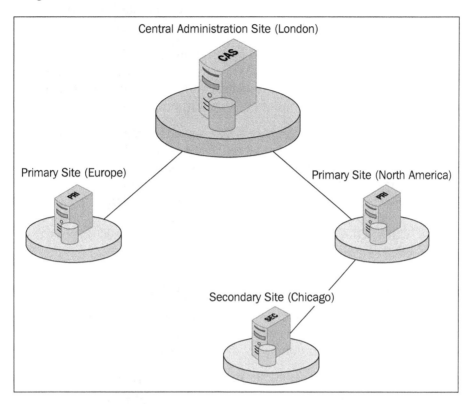

 Don't just let technology dictate your decisions we have just made a decision based on both technology and logical thinking. This is as important as making decisions for technical reasons.

High availability of the database or fault tolerance is not stated in the requirements but it is good practice to include a plan on how you would include this functionality, unless it has been explicitly excluded from the scope of the project. For our customer, they have not stated either way if this is or is not a requirement. For this reason, we will make some recommendations on high availability and fault tolerance.

Licensing is also a stated requirement, in that, if required, we should reduce it where possible. While we usually cannot do much in this area, System Center 2012 is one area where this can be addressed by looking at the SQL Server licensing.

You are allowed to deploy the SQL Server Standard edition with any System Center 2012 component provided it is the only SQL instance and no other databases are served out of the same server. For this the SQL Server Standard license cost will be included in the System Center 2012 license.

With this information, we need to now look at our usage of SQL Server and how the edition we select impacts our hierarchy. When we are deploying a hierarchy, the edition of SQL Server we deploy on the central administration site is the one that will determine how many clients our hierarchy can support.

When we deploy SQL Server Enterprise or Datacenter edition, the hierarchy can support a combined total of 400,000 devices. The Standard edition limits us to 50,000 clients; in this scenario, although SQL supports an in-place edition upgrade from standard to enterprise, Configuration Manager does not support this due to the way in which the database is partitioned. A primary site or secondary site in a hierarchy is not affected by the edition of SQL Server that is used for that site. However, a primary site with a SQL Server installed locally is limited to 50,000 clients; the limit with a remote SQL Server instance is 100,000 clients.

Planning for the SQL Server configuration

The information we have on how the SQL Server edition that we select affects the hierarchy and licensing presents us with a few choices for the configuration of SQL Server. We have four configuration options, which are laid out here:

- Deploy all site servers with SQL Server Enterprise edition
- Deploy all site servers with SQL Server Standard edition
- Deploy the central administration site with SQL Server Enterprise edition and all other sites with SQL Server Standard
- Deploy the central administration site with SQL Server Enterprise edition, all primary sites with SQL Server Standard, and use SQL Server Express for the secondary site

Now that we have several options available to us, we need to look at which is the best option. The first option is to deploy all site servers with the Enterprise edition of SQL Server. While this would be the most flexible option, it would also be the most expensive one as we would need four SQL Server enterprise licenses.

The next option is to deploy every site with the standard edition of SQL Server. This would be the most cost-effective option as it provides our whole hierarchy with SQL Server licenses, which are covered under the deployment of System Center 2012. However, it does leave the hierarchy restricted. This means that because we are deploying the standard edition of SQL Server on the central administration site, we can never have more than 50,000 clients in our hierarchy.

As we are already managing half of that limit, it would not be good planning once we add growth figures on for the hierarchy to leave it potentially short for the future.

The third option is much more attractive as this does not place a limitation on the size of our hierarchy, except for the 400,000 limit. What it means is that we only need one Enterprise edition license and the rest is covered under our existing agreement. This may seem perfect but what about the secondary site? A secondary site can run under SQL Server Express edition; better yet, this can be used all the way up to the 5,000 client limit of a secondary site.

Now that we know this, we can see that the most sensible option for scalability and cost is a balance between two of the options that we have. For our customer, we will recommend the fourth option as their SQL Server editions.

Planning for fault tolerance and high availability

One of our requirements is to reduce the server infrastructure used for the deployment of the hierarchy. Given this is a requirement, it would not be advisable to design our high availability around the database service, as this would introduce the need for a cluster, which would require additional servers.

In our customer's environment, as they are using a virtualization environment, it would make much more sense to make use of their existing replication technology or cluster. We will put our intent to use their existing infrastructure for our solution. This is also important as we want to make sure the correct amount of capacity is available.

Defining the business benefits

While infrastructure design documents are technical documents and in many cases very technical, they are often looked over by decision makers in both IT and finance. It is important that the top of your document includes a statement of what problem this design fixes and what business benefits it brings to the table.

Including this information at the top, from experience, gives the nontechnical readers of the document all the information they need to either sign off the design and provide the financial backing for the project or ask you to provide more information.

For our example customer, we have the following great benefits to add into the documentation, including the fact that we are answering all of the stated requirements:

- We have reduced the amount of infrastructure required to manage the same amount of clients
- Administration is much simpler with all administrators pointing to one single secure console where they can only see the objects in their department

- Administrators in London maintain full control over the full hierarchy and all of the clients within it

- We have provided a solution to manage the traffic between sites to address the speed of the link between London and New York

- Custom client settings can be easily deployed and managed from one single site rather than administering many sites

- We have provided an acceptable solution to enable the site to continue working if the virtualization host fails

- Then, finally, by looking at the licensing of SQL Server, we have saved a considerable amount of money required to license the SQL Server

When you write the business benefits in a document, remember who will read it. Try and put the financial benefits before and process or technical benefits as these will satisfy the reader of the document without them having to read much.

Delivering the design documentation

Now that we have decided on our design, we need to make sure our design is documented. Every design document is different based on the requirements but a few headings are listed, which will give some direction on the layout of the document:

- Project overview
- Requirements
- Risks
- Assumptions
- Solution overview
    - Physical network topology
    - Active Directory Domain environment
    - Server environment
    - Configuration Manager Architecture
    - Disaster Recovery
    - Sizing requirements

- Licensing overview
- Appendix: Licensing overview
- Appendix: Security accounts required
- Appendix: Anti-virus exclusions
- Appendix: Firewall port requirements

This will give you a good high-level design document with all the information that people need, including the decisions you have made to reach the design that you are setting out in the document. Consultancy companies as well often deliver detailed design documents, which include much more information and more detailed diagrams.

Design diagrams

Now that we have prepared our design documentation, we need to prepare our diagrams so people can see how our solution is put together at a graphical level. Diagrams can take many forms and be drawn up in many ways. The following diagrams are included with our design:

- ˙ General overview showing how the solution looks
- A diagram showing the solution with the components it interfaces with (for example, hypervisor, storage, network, Active Directory, and firewalls)
- A diagram showing policy, content, and database traffic flow between each site server and site system

Summary

In our opening chapter, we have learned how the Configuration Manager sites interact with each other and how implementing sites in different scenarios can have an impact on the hierarchy. We have also seen how you can manage multiple forests, which are both trusted and un-trusted in an effective and secured manner.

To finish off, we also looked at an example design scenario and went through the steps involved in making sure our design is fit for purpose, is scalable, and is also highly available. In the next chapter, we will take our hierarchy one step further and look at securing the environment using certificates.

2
Implementing Security with Certificates

One of the most overlooked subjects when setting up Configuration Manager is the need to implement security. The requirements for this are purely on a per-customer basis. Very few industries will require this level of encryption for this type of data, unless they are supporting Internet-facing clients. Regardless of whether you are using certificates or not, information in Configuration Manager can be signed and encrypted. This is very useful and usually satisfies the majority of security requirements.

If this is not the case for your implementation, then you need to look at using certificates. In this chapter, we will look at certificates in detail from top to bottom; this will include looking at the following topics:

- How to plan for certificates
- How to set up secure communication using PKI and HTTPS
- How to deploy certificates to domain joined workstations
- How to deploy certificates to workgroup workstations

Planning for the use of certificates

One of the great things about Configuration Manager is that it actually uses a combination of PKI certificates and self-signed certificates. The documentation advises that you should use certificates as a best practice. This is sound advice and you should follow this where possible; however, I have found that usually people are more than willing to accept what little risk there is of not running with certificates.

> Note that the setup of certificates is outside the scope of Configuration Manager and is not intended to replace a certificates specialist, as for troubleshooting you require deep knowledge of the setup of the certificate authority.

Certificates are required in some scenarios though; if you plan to use any one of the following features, then you are required to use certificates:

- Internet-based client management
- Management of mobile devices
- Management of Apple Mac devices
- Cloud distribution points
- Managing out of band computers with Intel AMT

You can use any certificate authority that supports the appropriate requirements for the certificates you require. I always like to use a Microsoft CA as it provides me with the ability to use autoenrolment for the client certificates when using an enterprise certificate authority. This becomes a very attractive solution when I need to deploy client certificates to any large number of devices. It also means that the certificates are centrally managed and the **certificate revocation list** (**CRL**) is also centrally managed.

When Configuration Manager detects that an appropriate certificate for use has been found, it will automatically use that certificate for communications. If a PKI certificate is not available for any reason, then a self-signed certificate will be generated by Configuration Manager instead.

> All the certificates that Configuration Manager can use must contain single-byte characters in the subject name or the subject alternative name.

Configuration Manager clients with certificates communicate with the appropriate site systems using HTTPS. This communication is encrypted using the industry standard SSL. Clients can also communicate using HTTP sometimes even when clients have certificates; these scenarios are as follows:

- When clients fall back to using HTTP after the client fails to communicate using HTTPS and the site system allows this configuration
- Communication with the following site system roles:
  - Fallback status point
  - PXE-enabled distribution point
  - Notification data sent to the management point

Setting up a secure communication

In the previous versions of Configuration Manager, setting up a secure communication on your site was often difficult and not very flexible in that we could only tell clients to communicate using one mode or another. This was known as mixed mode and native mode, which was set at a site level. With Configuration Manager 2012, these site modes have gone and site system roles now support communication with either HTTP or HTTPS depending on the configuration. This has been moved from the site configuration and makes it much easier to set up and deploy, even in live environments.

 Secure communication in Configuration Manager 2012 is a whole new ball game; the way we set up the site for secure communication is completely different from previous versions.

In this section, we will go through the entire setup process to have your client's communication with site system roles secure using HTTPS.

Preparing the certificate authority

In the examples here, we will be using Active Directory Certificate Services as part of a Windows Server 2012 R2 Active Directory Domain. The setup process is the same as in the previous versions; however, where applicable, differences will be highlighted.

Our lab environment where we will generate certificates is also running certificate services on the domain controller. This is not a good practice for a production environment, and you should always design your certificate authority in a secure manner that is recommended by the vendor. More information on setting up a Microsoft certificate authority can be found on TechNet at `http://bit.ly/1rgzWwK`.

As part of the certificate services installation, the following role services are also available:

- Certification authority
- Certificate enrollment policy web service
- Certificate enrollment web service
- Certification authority web enrolment service
- Network device enrollment service
- Online responder

We will only be deploying the certification authority in our environment; you may require others in your environment.

 Remember that certificate services is a service other applications can call upon; always take this into account when configuring the service. Work with your security team and other teams to ensure an existing certificate authority does not already exist.

Setting up certificate services using the user interface

Similar to most actions in Windows Server 2012 R2, from the Server Manager either navigate to **Manage** and **Add Roles and Features** or perform the same action from the **Quick Start** menu. On the **Add Roles and Features Wizard** window, as shown in the following screenshot, click on **Next** through all the wizard pages until you get to the **Server Roles** page. From here, tick **Active Directory Certificate Services**, accept the default options that appear, and then click on **Next** to skip onto the **Active Directory Certificate Services Role Services** page. The only option you should have ticked on the **Role Services** page is **Certification Authority**. In our environment for lab purposes, this is the only option we require.

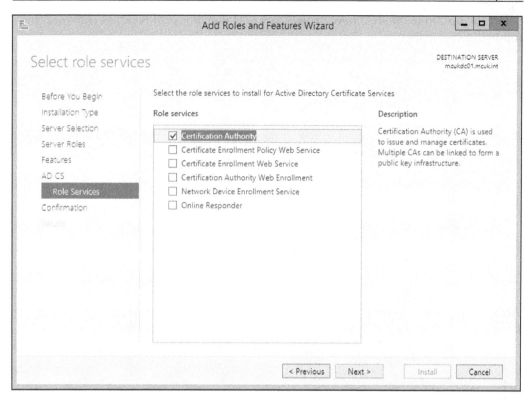

Click on **Next** to go to the confirmation page where you can press **Install** and let the certification authority install on your server. Depending on the configuration of your server, this should take no longer than one minute to complete.

On the completion screen, you should see a blue link in the middle of the screen that says **Configure Active Directory Certificate Services on the destination server**. Click on this link to begin the configuration of the role that we have just installed. In the following wizard, specify a domain account. The screen provides you with information on the permissions required by the account. Then, click on **Next**.

Tick the box for the **Certification Authority** option on the **Role Services** screen and then click on **Next**. Make sure the setup type is **Enterprise CA** and the CA type is **Root CA**. Click on **Next**.

Select the option to create a new private key and then click on **Next**, as shown in the following screenshot:

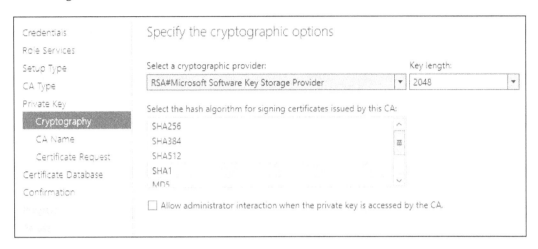

Accept the default options all the way through to the confirmation screen. Review the options on the screen, and when you are happy, click on **Configure**.

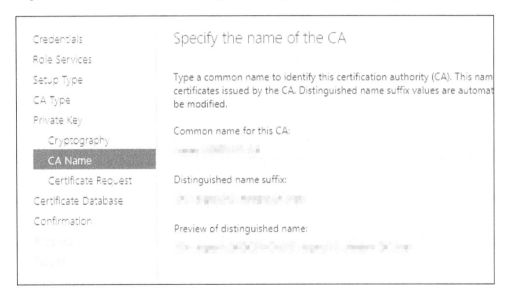

Again, depending on the configuration of your server, this should take no longer than one minute to complete. Click on **Close** twice to close down the configuration and role installation screens. At this point, you can also close Server Manager. Certificate services have now been installed and configured on your server.

Setting up certificate services using PowerShell

If you prefer to use PowerShell, then you can also use it to set up certificate services on your server. Simply launch the PowerShell prompt as an administrator and type the following command to make sure the server manager module is available:

```
Import-Module ServerManager
```

Once this command has been executed, run the following command from the same window to install the certificate authority feature:

```
Add-WindowsFeature Adcs-Cert-Authority
```

When the feature has been installed, we need to configure the feature just like when we use the user interface. In the same window as the previous two commands, execute the following command:

```
Install-AdcsCertificationAuthority -CAType EnterpriseRootCa
-CryptoProviderName "RSA#Microsoft Software Key Storage Provider"
-KeyLength 2048 -HashAlgorithmName SHA1 -ValidityPeriod Years
-ValidityPeriodUnits 5
```

PowerShell is a fantastic way to automate how you deploy services and servers. Consider using PowerShell where possible to keep your setup consistent.

Configuring certificate templates

Configuration Manager might require a number of certificate templates for a number of different uses. Here, we will look at the configuration of some of the most common certificates used in Configuration Manager. Before we look at this, you will need a security group in Active Directory called **CM IIS Servers**. If you have a standard naming convention for security groups, then feel free to adopt that format for this group.

In this group, add any servers that have or will have IIS installed to perform functionality for Configuration Manager, such as a distribution point or management point. This security group will be used to provide permission to certificate templates to ensure only the correct servers have access to provision the certificate.

A full guide to deploying the rest of the certificates other than the ones noted here can be found on TechNet at http://technet.microsoft.com/en-us/library/ gg682023.aspx.

Creating the web server certificate template

Open the **Certificate Authority** console and navigate to the **Certificate Templates** node, right-click in the pane displayed and click on **Manage**. This will open the certificate template console where the template will be created. Right-click on the certificate template called **Web Server** and click on **Duplicate**.

Always ensure that your certificate templates are created with Windows Server 2003, Enterprise Edition as the compatibility settings or the default options if you are using Windows Server 2012.

In the **General** tab of the new template properties, enter CM Web Server Certificate as the template display name, as shown in the following screenshot. In the **Subject Name** tab, ensure that **Supply in the request** is also selected.

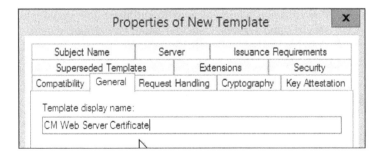

Permissions for both domain administrators and enterprise administrators should not have the **Enroll** option ticked. Finally, add the security group that you have created and ensure this group has the **Read** and **Enroll** permissions selected. No other permissions are required.

Click on **OK** to close the **Properties** window, which will also create the new template. This certificate is now ready to be marked for issuing.

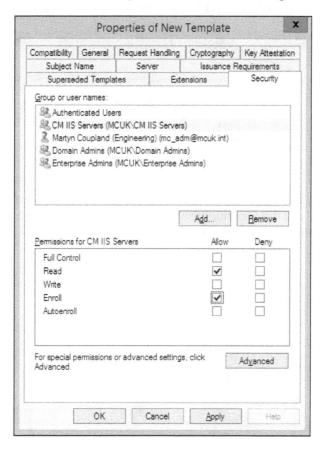

Creating the client certificate for distribution points

Open the **Certificate Authority** console and navigate to the **Certificate Templates** node; right-click on the pane displayed and click on **Manage**. This will open the certificate template console where the template will be created. Right-click on the certificate template called **Workstation Authentication** and click on **Duplicate**.

 Always ensure that your certificate templates are created with Windows Server 2003, Enterprise Edition as the compatibility settings or the default options if you are using Windows Server 2012.

In the **General** tab of the new template properties, enter CM Client DP Certificate as the template display name, as shown in the following screenshot. In the **Request Handling** tab, ensure that **Allow private key to be exported** is also selected.

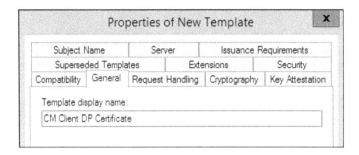

In the **Security** tab, for enterprise administrators ensure that the **Enroll** permission is not ticked. Finally, add the security group that you have created and ensure this group has the **Read** and **Enroll** permissions selected. No other permissions are required.

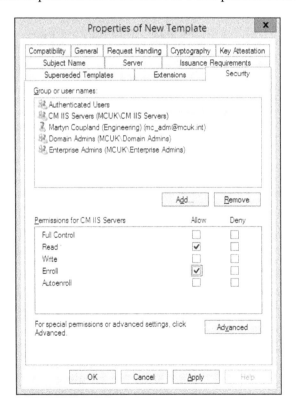

Click on **OK** to close the **Properties** window, which will also create the new template. This certificate is now ready to be marked for issuing.

Creating the client certificate for Windows computers

Open the **Certificate Authority** console and navigate to the **Certificate Templates** node, right-click in the pane displayed, and click on **Manage**. This will open the certificate template console where the template will be created. Right-click on the certificate template called **Workstation Authentication** and click on **Duplicate**.

 Always ensure that your certificate templates are created with Windows Server 2003, Enterprise Edition as the compatibility settings or the default options if you are using Windows Server 2012.

In the **General** tab of the new template properties, enter CM Client Certificate as the template display name, as shown in the following screenshot. In the **Security** tab, for domain computers make sure that **Autoenroll** and **Enroll** are ticked as well as **Read**.

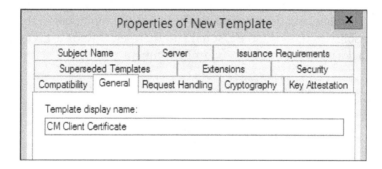

These permissions ensure that computers can automatically obtain the certificate when set up via group policy. This negates the need for you to manually issue a workstation certificate to every Windows computer where you install the Configuration Manager agent.

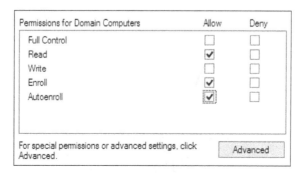

Click on **OK** to close the **Properties** window, which will also create the new template. This certificate is now ready to be marked for issuing.

Issuing certificate templates

When all your certificate templates have been created, you need to issue these so that they can be requested by the appropriate client devices and servers. Open the **Certificate Authority** console and navigate to the **Certificate Templates** node. Right-click on the certificate templates, select **New**, and then select **Certificate Templates to Issue**.

Select multiple certificates by using the *Ctrl* key and clicking on the certificates. Once you have selected all of the certificates, click on **OK**. These certificates are now ready to be enrolled by workstations and clients.

Requesting the web server certificate

On each IIS server, go to **Start** and then **Run**. Type `certlm.msc` to open the **Certificates** console, this should automatically connect to the local computer. You can verify this by checking the contents of the text at the top node on the left-hand side of the console. Right-click on **Personal** and then select **Request New Certificate** from the **All tasks** option. Select the default enrolment policy.

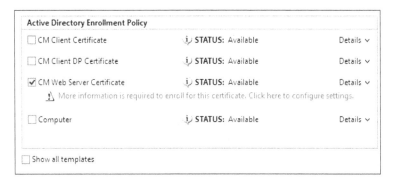

Tick the **CM Web Server Certificate** checkbox; you will notice that under the certificate a warning triangle is displayed. This is because the certificate requires additional information before you can enroll for it. Click on the link below the certificate to begin the configuration of the certificate.

 You can also enroll certificates using PowerShell. There is a great reference on how to perform this action on TechNet at `http://bit.ly/1zbc2r0`.

Under the **Subject** tab, select **DNS** from the **Type** dropdown under **Alternative name**, as shown in the following screenshot; enter all the possible scenarios for the name of the server. This includes FQDN and also any Internet names if the server is Internet facing.

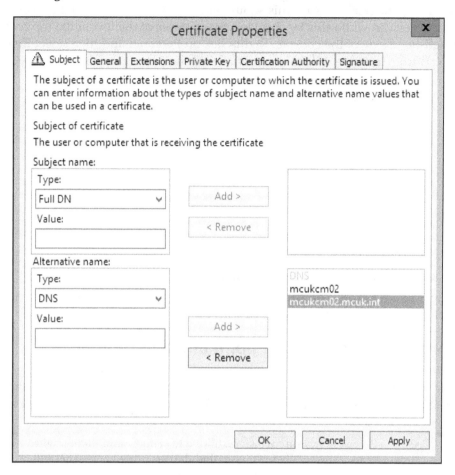

Once this information has been entered and verified, click on **OK**. You will then be returned to the enrollment page where you can click on the **Enroll** button to obtain the certificate. Now in the personal certificate store, you should see the certificate we have just provisioned.

Requesting the client certificate for distribution points

On the distribution point server, go to **Start** and then to **Run**. Type `certlm.msc` to open the **Certificates** console; this should automatically connect to the local computer. You can verify this by checking the contents of the text at the top node on the left-hand side of the console. Right-click on **Personal** and then select **Request New Certificate** from the **All tasks** option. Select the default enrolment policy.

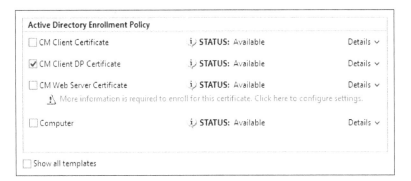

Tick the **CM Client DP Certificate** checkbox from the list of available certificates, and then click on **Enroll**. You should then see the certificate in the personal certificate store for the local system and not the current user.

Exporting the distribution point client certificate

Once the certificate has been enrolled by the server, you need to export the certificate so it can then be imported into Configuration Manager. Select the certificate that you have just provisioned; right-click on the certificate and select **Export** from **All tasks**.

 If you are not sure which certificate to export, scroll to the right of the console where you can find the certificate name. This will help you determine which certificate to export.

To export the certificate, the following process should be followed.

1. On the **Export Private Key** page, check the option to allow the private key to be exported.

2. On the **Export File Format** page, ensure that the option **Personal Information Exchange - PKCS #12 (.PFX)** is checked; this will ensure that the format of the export is correct.

3. On the **Password** page, specify a password to protect the exported certificate with the private key, and then click on **Next**.

4. On the **File to Export** page, specify the name of the file that you want to export, and then click on **Next**.

 You should consider storing the password for the certificate in a password safe, for example, or at another safe location.

Deploying the client certificate for Windows workstations

Create a new group policy object and give the policy an appropriate name. Open the policy to edit it, expand **Policies under Computer Configuration**. From here, expand the nodes to the Windows Settings/Security Settings/ Public Key Policies path.

From here, open the **Certificate Services Client – Auto-enrollment** object by selecting **Properties**. Configure the options as shown in the following screenshot, ensure the configuration model is set to **Enabled**, and then make sure both of the checkboxes are ticked:

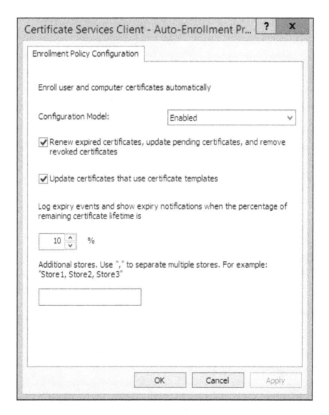

Make sure this group policy is linked; assign any security that you might want for the group policy object. The next time a workstation reboots, the policy will take effect and clients should automatically enroll the certificate.

Configuring IIS to use the distribution point certificate

Once the certificate for the distribution point is provisioned, you need to configure IIS to use the certificate. Open the IIS Manager and navigate to the default website. On the actions pane below the right-hand side of the console, select **Bindings**.

From the **Site Bindings** screen, select the HTTPS binding (port 443 by default) and select **Edit**, as shown in the following screenshot:

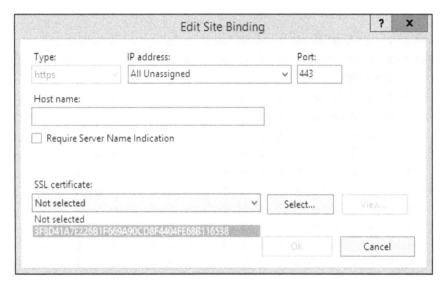

Select the certificate from the list of available certificates. If you have more than one certificate listed, click on the **Select** button where you can view more details on the certificates available to IIS.

Click on **OK** once you have selected the certificate and then click on **Close**. You can now close IIS Manager. You can verify that the certificate is working correctly by browsing to `https://servername/` (replacing `servername` with the name of your site system role you have installed the certificate on). Make sure you test all the DNS names that you entered when you provisioned the certificate to verify it is working properly. Your browser should show no certificate warnings and display something similar to the following screenshot:

 You can use the same certificate here for a management point as well as a distribution point. The process is the same for provisioning the certificate as well as for configuring IIS.

Configuring Configuration Manager

To begin configuring your Configuration Manager site to start using secure communication, you will require a CER file of your root CA. The file you export must be a DER X.509 certificate.

In the administration workspace, expand the site configuration node and select **Sites**. Right-click on your site and then select **Properties**. In the **Client Computer Communication** tab, you have the ability to set options on how clients communicate with your site.

Import your root CA certificate by clicking on **Set** at the bottom of the window. You can import multiple root certificates if required. This functionality supports environments that may have multiple certificate authorities.

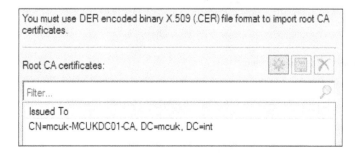

The certificates you specify here will be used to verify the certificate chain of any certificates configured in the hierarchy. You are recommended to make sure that your clients are properly communicating with a HTTP management point and distribution point as well as software update point before setting your site to communicate purely in HTTPS.

Tick the box labeled **Use PKI client certificate where available**. This will instruct clients to communicate with the site if they have the correct certificate.

Once you have confirmed that all clients are communicating with the site using HTTPS, you may switch the communication mode from **HTTPS** or **HTTP** to **HTTPS** only.

If you have a mix of HTTP and HTTPS management points, then clients will select HTTPS management points as a preference over HTTP, as shown in the following screenshot:

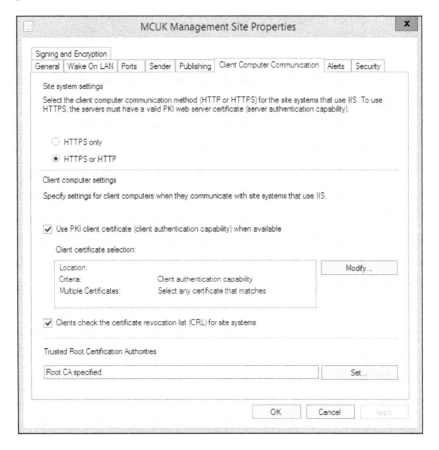

Configuring distribution points to use certificates

In the distribution point properties in the **Servers and Site System Roles** node, find your distribution point server and double-click on the distribution point object. In the **General** tab, at the bottom of the screen, you can switch from a self-signed certificate to import a certificate.

Here, you can specify the path to your exported distribution point client certificate and enter the password associated when the certificate was exported. This will enable the distribution point to use the client certificate created from your certificate authority rather than the default self-signed certificate, as shown in the following screenshot:

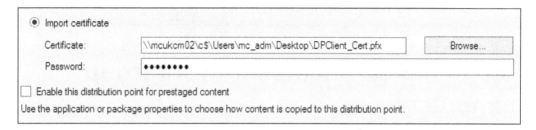

You can then click on **OK** to save the changes; this action will configure your certificate for you. You can change the certificate if required at any time or switch back to a self-signed certificate should it be required.

 If you switch back to a self-signed certificate, make sure you clean up any existing certificates as a best practice.

Configuring management points to use certificates

Management points require very little configuration to make, in this case, use HTTPS communication. Once IIS has been configured to use the web server certificate from the certificate authority, open the management point properties in the **Servers and Site System Roles** node, find your management point server, and double-click on the management point object.

In the **General** tab, simply select the **HTTPS** radio button and save the changes by clicking on **OK**, as shown in the following screenshot:

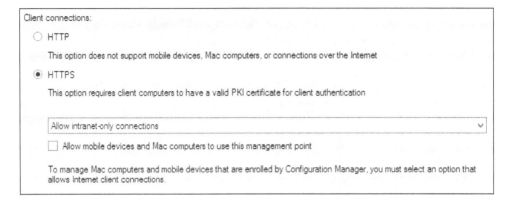

Deploying certificates to workgroup computers

You can still use your certificates from your internal certificate authority on workgroup computers. When clients are on the domain, we use autoenrolment to make sure our clients get the correct certificate.

While not as intuitive and simple as deploying certificates on the domain, however, we can use a script to first generate the certificate request. The next code does just that. First of all, we need to define the client name; this should be entered to make sure the certificate request is correct.

The next section of code generates the certificate request as well as saying what the template is. The certificate will generate a new certificate and then export the created certificate. Lines that require editing have been highlighted; this script should be executed as an administrator:

```
set subjectname=client.fqdn.co.uk
echo Generating INF file for certificate
echo ;————CertificateRequestTemplate.inf———- >> %subjectname%.inf
echo [NewRequest]                                    >> %subjectname%.inf
echo Subject="cn=%subjectname%"                      >> %subjectname%.inf
echo Exportable=TRUE                                 >> %subjectname%.inf
echo KeyLength=2048                                  >> %subjectname%.inf
```

```
echo KeySpec=1                       ;key exchange                          >>
%subjectname%.inf
echo KeyUsage=0xA0                                                          >>
%subjectname%.inf
echo MachineKeySet=TRUE                                                     >>
%subjectname%.inf
echo [RequestAttributes]                                                    >>
%subjectname%.inf
echo CertificateTemplate="ConfigMgrClientCertificate" ; this is for
Client Authentication     >> %subjectname%.inf
echo SAN="DNS=%subjectname%"                              >>
%subjectname%.inf

echo Generating certificate request
CertReq -New -f %subjectname%.inf %subjectname%.req
echo Retrieving certificate
CertReq -Submit -q -f -config <CAServerName.FQDN.CO.UK>\<CA-NAME-CA>
%subjectname%.req %subjectname%.cer
Echo Importing certificate
certreq -accept %subjectname%.cer
Echo Exporting certificate
Certutil -f -p <password> -exportpfx %subjectname% .\
certs\%subjectname%.pfx
certutil -delstore "MY" %subjectname%
del %subjectname%.req
del %subjectname%.inf
del %subjectname%.cer
echo Completed!
```

To put this all together, we will need a copy of our root certificate. We will also need a copy of the client binary files. Putting them all on a USB stick is the best method as you can keep them all in one place and it makes it portable.

Our final bit of code will add the trusted root certificate to the trusted root certificate store; import our client certificate created in the preceding code. Then, finally execute the client installation. Lines that require editing have been highlighted; this script should be run as an administrator:

```
Echo Adding Trusted Root Certificate
certutil -addstore -f "ROOT" "%~dp0MyTrustedRoot.cer"
echo Import Client Certificate
Certutil -p agoodpassword -importpfx "%~dp0certs\%computername%.pfx"
echo Install ConfigMgr Client
"%~dp0\client\ccmsetup.exe" /source:%~dp0certs\client /
mp:myserver.fqdn.co.uk /usePKICert /NOCRLCheck SMSSITECODE=ZZZ
CCMHOSTNAME=sccmserver.fqdn.co.uk
Echo Finished
```

The folder structure for your USB drive is simple as well. Here is an example of how the layout should look:

- Client: This is the folder that contains your client binary files
- Certs: These are the PFX certificates for the computer
- GenerateCertificate.cmd: This is the first script shown in this section
- InstallClient.cmd: This is the second script shown in the preceding code
- RootCert.cer: This is the root certificate from your CA

Summary

In this chapter, we have explored the world of using certificates to secure our Configuration Manager environment. We have gone through the high-level process of setting up a test certificate authority and configuring the certificate templates.

It is also possible to set Configuration Manager so clients can sign and encrypt communication to their management point. If implementing certificates is overkill for you, this is also a good security step.

We also looked at the configuration steps involved to let Configuration Manager know about our certificates and enable our clients to communicate with our site using the certificates we have generated.

Finally, we explored how to generate certificates to use for our workgroup clients where we cannot use the domain to automatically enroll the certificates. In the next chapter, we will look at how to use inventory to our advantage and how to configure the inventory to work for us.

3
Working with Inventory, Asset Intelligence, and Software Metering

Probably one of the biggest uses for Configuration Manager is the collection of both hardware and software inventory from your clients. For most customers, this feature is turned on by default and left with the default settings.

The same can be said for software metering. It is a part of Configuration Manager that is well-known, but people do not always utilize it properly or to its full potential. This can be due to restrictions in your country or because you need the permission of your human resources department. We can say exactly the same for asset intelligence as well.

In this chapter, we will explore the use of all three functions and look at the following sections in more detail to gain a better understanding of how to make inventory, asset intelligence, and software metering work for you.

- Configuring software and hardware inventory
- Using inventory data to your advantage
- Making use of software metering
- Real-world use of asset intelligence
- Controlling applications with inventory data

Configuring the software and hardware inventory

Once you have installed your site, it is true that you are not required to complete any configuration to start collecting inventory. For software inventory, though, you will need to define some rules to start collecting data. Without any configuration, inventory will work and collect the default set of inventory from your clients.

The implementation of any feature is as important to the success of the deployment as the design of the hierarchy. For this reason, you should always plan and design each aspect of your configuration; inventory is no exception to this.

 To really take advantage of the power of inventory, look at what extra inventory you might want to collect, and how often you want to collect it. Configuration is as important as design.

Planning the configuration of inventory

The first step in this process is to look at the default policy. In Configuration Manager, policies are merged and in the event of conflicting settings, the priority is used to resolve the conflict. This means that you must think about what you want set in your policy as this is where we set inventory configuration.

 In Configuration Manager 2012 R2, you can use the resultant set of client settings functionality that can help with troubleshooting by showing you how the policy settings are merged.

We must think about what types of devices we will be managing in the hierarchy; what are the primary requirements for the hierarchy? Can we turn inventory off if we are not going to utilize the data it collects? These questions have an impact on the design of the site and the size requirements for the database.

Configuring the hardware inventory

Try and make your default policy as generic as possible. This way, you can create policies for different types of devices, for example, which are more bespoke and collect exactly the information you require. Examples of this might include data such as whether you want to collect inventory more often on client operating systems and less often on servers.

In the following steps, we are going to build some policies to manage desktops and laptops as well as servers. We have different requirements for these operating systems. Let's have a look at these requirements, first of all for servers:

- Server features
- Disk quotas
- Share information

The following information should not be collected on servers:

- Power management
- Recently used applications

Now, the requirements for the desktop inventory are as follows:

- App-V client information
- USB devices
- Quick-fix engineering
- Boot configuration data

The following information is not required in the desktop inventory:

- CD-ROM
- TPM
- BitLocker

BitLocker and TPM information is required for laptop devices though.

For scheduling, servers should have inventory performed every five days and laptops and desktops every two days. On all other devices, such as mobile devices, inventory should be collected every seven days.

Configuring the required settings

Now that we have the requirements from the customer, we can start to implement these requirements. We have the following four clear policies that we need to create:

- Server policy
- Desktop policy
- Laptop policy
- Mobile device policy

As the requirements for laptops and desktops differ, we need to create different policies. If the requirements were the same, then we could simply have two policies, one for servers and one for workstations, for example.

What this means for the default policy based on the requirements is that we can make this policy generic for all other devices. For example, we can disable the collection of information for mobile devices and any other information that is not common over all platforms.

In our example, we are just using the policies to override inventory settings. What is great about policies in Configuration Manager is the ability to override sections of the policy. This is good for us as we are only interested in software and hardware inventory. Any items of the policy that are not fulfilled by custom policies are filled with the default settings from the default policy; this is why the default policy has a priority of 10,000 as it will always be the last to apply.

To start compiling a policy to match our requirements for servers, create a new device settings policy in the **Administration** workspace under the **Client Settings** node. For the name of the policy, enter `Server Policy`, as shown in the following screenshot:

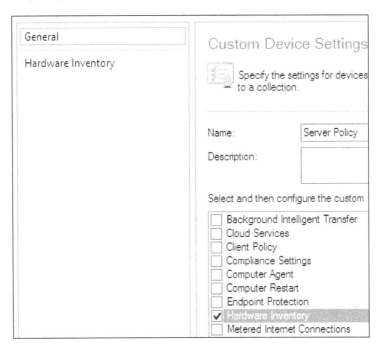

Then, from the list of policy categories that are listed underneath, tick **Hardware Inventory**. This should now be listed in the left-hand side of the window, which is open. Click on the item on the left-hand side to begin editing the policy settings.

To help keep the database size under control, make sure that you uncheck anything that you do not require. It can always be checked later if you need to start collecting that information.

Given the requirements for our server policy, we need to tick the following WMI classes to ensure the information is included in the inventory for these devices:

- `Win32_DiskQuota`
- `Win32_ServerFeature`

We can also uncheck the following WMI classes from the same window as they are not required:

- **Power management**
- **Recently used applications**

Before we configure these, let's configure the schedule details. We need the schedule for servers to be set to collect inventory every five days. Click on the **Schedule** button on the screen and set the schedule as defined and click on **OK**.

Now that we have configured the schedule, we can go ahead and select the classes that are required and uncheck those that are not. You can also, in this window, connect to a remote computer and browse the WMI to select the class and properties that you want from a remote machine.

 If you have a **Managed Object Format** (**MOF**) file from previous versions of Configuration Manager, you can also import the MOF using the **Import** button.

In the following screenshot, you can see an example of where a custom MOF file has been imported:

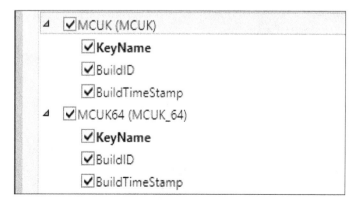

When you have set the classes that are required, click on **OK** to create the custom policy. After the policy has been created, you can go ahead and deploy the policy you have created to a collection, which contains the devices you require.

Any device collection can be targeted for device-based client settings; the same is true for user collections when working with user policies. Where possible, try and use a query that selects devices based on the operating system caption. You can use wildcards as well to look for every operating system caption that contains the word server. This process can be repeated for each of the requirements that we have listed.

Initiating inventory cycles manually

As you know, inventory in Configuration Manager is triggered on a scheduled basis. This is done for good reason, but sometimes you might want to manually trigger the schedule to run. This can be done with PowerShell, and it is really simple to do. The following code snippet is all you need. Don't forget to run the PowerShell console as an administrator. Note that the client needs to download policy information after the settings are deployed before running software or hardware inventory.

```
$SMSClient = [wmiclass] ("\\.\root\ccm:SMS_Client")
$SMSClient.TriggerSchedule("{00000000-0000-0000-0000-000000000001}")
```

The preceding code snippet works for hardware inventory. The same can be done with software inventory as well; the code is the same but this time we just change the schedule ID:

```
$SMSClient = [wmiclass] ("\\.\root\ccm:SMS_Client")
$SMSClient.TriggerSchedule("{00000000-0000-0000-0000-000000000002}")
```

 You can also use the same (preceding) script to trigger other schedules, such as a policy refresh or a software updates scan. All you need is the schedule ID.

In order to obtain the schedule ID, you can use the following snippet of PowerShell, which will display a list of schedules:

```
get-wmiobject CCM_Scheduler_ScheduledMessage `
-namespace root\ccm\policy\machine\actualconfig |
select-object ScheduledMessageID, TargetEndPoint |
where-object {$_.TargetEndPoint -ne "direct:execmgr"}
```

Once the manual schedule has completed, check the MP_Hinv.log and dataldr.log files on the server. This works well if you want to speed up your inventory for testing. In a production environment though, try and stay away from using this on a frequent basis, especially in an environment with lots of clients.

Using the inventory data to your advantage

By storing hardware and software inventory, you are storing a huge amount of information about the devices in your environment, which can be used for numerous purposes. Common examples of how this data is used are as follows:

- Automated removal of software
- License compliance for your estate
- Tracking the life of the assets

Making use of the inventory you collect is important for a number of reasons: the main reason is pure administration of your estate. For the preceding reasons, the inventory allows you to control your environment.

The way companies use inventory data varies; some companies use reporting to provide data for key performance indicators, while others just use the data for internal consumption within the team for anything from client health to what files are installed on the machine.

Controlling the inventory with control files

You can prevent software inventory from being processed against a folder using a control file. Similar to the no_sms_on_drive.sms file, you can create a file to prevent Configuration Manager site server components from getting installed to a drive. You can use the skpswi.dat file to prevent software inventory for the specific drive or folder.

Simply place the hidden file in the root of the location that you want to exclude; for example, the root of the c: drive will exclude software inventory for the full drive or the source share for your packages and applications.

You cannot do the same for hardware inventory as this is done on WMI classes; if you wish to exclude information from hardware inventory, then you need to create a policy that overrides this information for specific devices or remove it from the default policy.

 Software inventory is far slower to run than hardware inventory and it will consume much more space; you should pinpoint the files you are looking for rather than using wildcards.

Tracking assets with the inventory

It is very common these days for organizations to enter a lease agreement with a hardware vendor to provide them with devices for a set period, before they are refreshed after a certain period with newer equipment.

A vital part of this process is the management of devices from an inventory perspective. This includes knowing what hardware is in the chassis, and how long the device has been deployed. This information becomes even more important when you use System Center 2012 Service Manager, for example, where you can use Configuration Manager as a feed for the configuration management database.

Tracking the right information is essential as well to ensure you have the information needed to fulfill your lease agreement. Information that is common to collect includes:

- Motherboard
- Memory
- Graphics card
- Network cards
- Monitor information
- Serial numbers

Each of the preceding objects join to make a device; each of the objects in their own right in configuration management is a configuration item. Each of these configuration items build up into a system, which requires tracking.

Let's have a look at some of the hardware classes in WMI, which we will need to collect to gain this information for reporting purposes:

- `Win32_Baseboard`
- `Win32_Battery`
- `Win32_CDROMDrive`
- `Win32_ComputerSystem`
- `Win32_DiskDrive`
- `Win32_PhysicalMemory`
- `Win32_Processor`
- `Win32_SCSIController`
- `Win32_SystemEnclosure`
- `Win32_VideoController`

All of these classes can be really useful to get a solid picture of what is in each of your devices. Collecting this information can also help you determine the changes that a device has experienced. This can help you fill in the gaps in a device's history, for example, someone may miss noting down a change to the video card in a device. This could potentially cause issues when it comes to returning the equipment to the vendor.

Tracking build cycles with the registry

It may be common as well for a tattoo or marker to be added to the registry for instance, such as the deployment date of the device. This can allow you to custom report via custom inventory entries to report on when devices are not just due a refreshed build image but potentially recalled early to be swapped out.

 As with any modification to built-in configuration files, always make a backup before you edit the file.

First, what information is useful for this reporting? A good starting point would be the ID of the build, and this could be anything. In this example, let's use a traditional GUID. Next is the time the machine was built. Using operating system deployment, this is easy to achieve. For simplicity, we can also use a UNIX timestamp, which is the number of seconds since January 1, 1970. Again, this is easy to generate in a script and add in to our task sequence.

Preparing the MOF files

In order to obtain the correct information for the MOF files we need, use the brilliant tool from Mark Cochrane, which is available at `http://bit.ly/Uy9pjH` and allows you to browse the registry for the individual key and values that you want and outputs the correct information for the modification of `configuration.mof` and for the import wizard in the inventory settings.

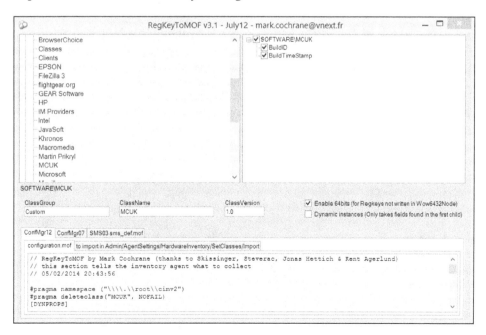

Simply browse to the key you require, select the values that you wish from the right-hand side, and make sure the **ClassName** value is something meaningful (without spaces). At the bottom of the screen are two tabs, one for the configuration MOF and another for the set classes import.

First of all, browse to `<install location>\inboxes\clifiles.src\hinv`; here, make a copy of your `configuration.mof` file. Next, open the MOF file to edit, and scroll right to the bottom of the file; you will see two tags named `added extensions start` and `added extensions end`. In between these tags, copy the whole of the contents from the first tab and paste it into this section.

Import custom modifications

Before you save the file, open the log file `<install location>\logs\dataldr.log`. When you save the file, you will notice that entries in this log saying your edits have been accepted. If, for some reason, the changes are not accepted, then double-check whether you have copied everything. You should see some lines in your log similar to what is shown in the following screenshot:

```
Configuratin.Mof change detected
Compiling MOF files and converting to policy.
Start of cimv2\sms\inv_config-to-policy conversion
Running MOFCOMP on C:\Program Files\Microsoft Configuration Manager\inboxes\clifiles.src\hinv\configuration.mof
MOF backed up to C:\Program Files\Microsoft Configuration Manager\data\hinvarchive\configuration.mof.bak
Successfully updated configuration.mof in the database.
```

From the second tab in the utility, again copy the contents to a Notepad window and save the file as a MOF file. Then, browse to the default policy (this is important), open the policy, and then select **Set Classes** from the hardware inventory category.

Select the MOF file that you just saved. Once this has been imported, you should be presented with a screen that looks like the following screenshot:

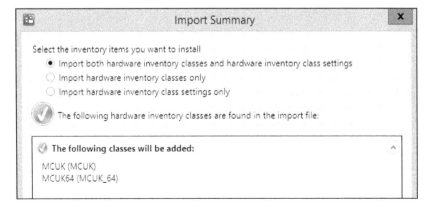

If everything is OK, then click on **Import**. When you are returned back to the classes screen, you should see the classes you have selected. By default, they will be checked, so make sure you uncheck them before saving the changes.

Next, in your policy where you want the registry key to be collected, open the policy and browse to **Set Classes** again in the hardware inventory category:

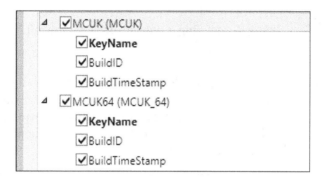

When this has been completed, you can verify it in the `dataldr.log` file; you can look for the client's inventory coming in. Once it has passed through this log, you will be able to use the Resource Explorer to find the information that has been inventoried as well as run queries against the data and also against the reports.

 Depending on the settings you have defined, this information will not be available until the client has retrieved the updated policy and has performed the next inventory cycle.

Tracking with reports

Reports are a vital part of Configuration Manager for many aspects. The inventory is where reporting becomes really powerful with all the data that is held about clients. Configuration Manager contains many useful built-in reports that can be used to help you track your assets.

Most of the hardware reports will be useful to let you query this information. You could even create a custom report, which shows all the information you need in one report; create a dashboard with graphs or dials for a summary of information.

Making use of software metering

Software metering is again a part of Configuration Manager that is well known but potentially not used to its full potential. By default, software metering rules are automatically created and disabled for a specific file, where more than 10 percent of the hierarchy have run the file.

 Software metering is only available for the full Windows client.

If the rule you require is already available, which is fairly likely, then it is just a case of right-clicking on the rule and selecting **Enable**. You can also create your own custom software metering rules. Again the process for this is simple. In the following screenshot, I have selected CMTrace.exe as the target for the rule. Once the file has been selected, the rest of the fields are populated.

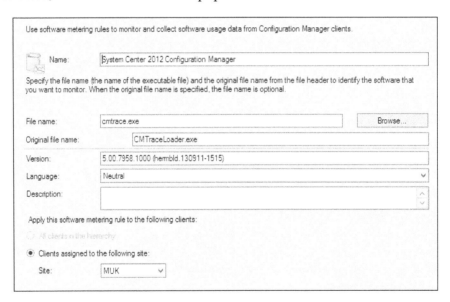

When you have completed the wizard, the rule will be created on the site you specify at the bottom of the screen. Once the rule has been created, you can then see the rule in the list of software metering rules, just like what is shown in the following screenshot:

Just like rules can be enabled by right-clicking, rules can also be disabled in the same way; simply right-click on the rule and select **Disable**. This will prevent any more data from getting collected.

Modifying metering retention

As with automatic rule generation, the setting that controls how long data is retained for is set by default. You can find this option in **Software Metering Properties** in the **Software Metering** node in the **Assets and Compliance** workspace. The setting by default is 90 days. For most customers, this is the correct value; you are unlikely to need to change this.

You may even want the data retention setting to reduce; there is no golden rule for this value, and most organizations do not even know that the setting exists. You may want to extend it for internal or regulatory compliance reasons.

Viewing metering data

Reports are available for administrators to view metering data that is stored in the database. Information will not be available until a number of summary maintenance tasks have run out of the box; Configuration Manager contains 13 reports, which give you all that you need to know about the usage of software on your environment.

One of the best reports is **Computers that have a metered program installed but have not run the program since a specified date**. This report allows you to view information on computers that have the metered program installed on their system, but have not run the program in the past few (specified number of) days.

One thing that is lacking from the console is the ability to manually set off a task to summarize the metering data; this will automatically run on a schedule in a maintenance task. You can download the Configuration Manager 2012 Toolkit, which contains a file `runmetersumm.exe` in the `Server tools` folder. If you pass the parameter of your database, you will kick off a manual process.

Removing unused software with metering data

This is a very common target that most organizations want to achieve. The simple result of this example is that it shows a collection of machines that have our application installed but have not executed it in the past so many days. In this example, we will say the past 30 days.

As with a lot of things in Configuration Manager, this is just one way to perform this task; you can use other methods too. This, however, seems to produce the most consistent results in line with the report.

The first thing we need to do here is create a collection that contains the machines that have executed our metered application in the last 30 days. This will be our control collection to contain these members, and we will reference this collection at a later date. The following query should be used as a query rule to select the right computers:

```
SELECT SMS_R_SYSTEM.ResourceID,
SMS_R_SYSTEM.ResourceType,
SMS_R_SYSTEM.Name,
SMS_R_SYSTEM.SMSUniqueIdentifier,
SMS_R_SYSTEM.ResourceDomainORWorkgroup,
SMS_R_SYSTEM.Client
FROM SMS_R_SYSTEM INNER JOIN SMS_MonthlyUsageSummary ON SMS_R_SYSTEM.
ResourceID = SMS_MonthlyUsageSummary.ResourceID
INNER JOIN SMS_MeteredFiles ON SMS_MonthlyUsageSummary.FileID = SMS_
MeteredFile.MeteredFileID
WHERE DateDiff(day, SMS_MonthlyUsageSummary.LastUsage, GetDate()) < 30
AND SMS_MeteredFiles.RuleID = XX
```

You can see in the preceding query that we simply need to change 30 to the number of days we want to check; we also need the rule ID for the software metering rule. You can easily get the ID for the metering rule by clicking on the rule in the software metering node. Select the rule you require and the information banner at the bottom of the screen will show the **Internal Rule ID**, as shown in the following screenshot:

Microsoft® Visual Studio® 2005 - csc.exe - 8.0. (1033)

Summary

Original File Name:	csc.exe
File Name:	csc.exe
Language:	English (United States)
Site Code:	MUK
Internal Rule ID:	16778218

The second collection is again simple to set up. In this collection, we can use the collection that we have previously created and a new query to find all the machines with our executable from the inventory. By design, we are selecting machines that have the executable available and then excluding the previous collection that lists machines, which have executed the metering rule in the past 30 days. What is left is machines that have the executable present but have not run the software in the past 30 days. This should be the same output as the report previously mentioned.

The following screenshot shows you an example of how this looks in the membership page of the collection wizard:

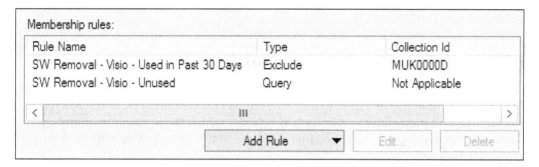

It is this collection that we have just created, using the power of the application model in Configuration Manager, where we can deploy an uninstall task to the collection to automate the removal of the software.

 If a system has both an install and uninstall for the same application deployed, then the install wins.

You can see here that we have created a deployment for unused instances of Mozilla Firefox:

Real-world use of asset intelligence

Asset intelligence is another feature in the stack of inventory and software data that is largely unused. The feature comes from a vast online catalog of software identifiers, which synchronizes with your site via the asset intelligence sync point.

Not only does this functionality provide you with a huge list of software families and categories, which categorizes software titles in the asset intelligence reports, but also gives you a list of hardware requirements for over 100 applications. You can run reports of your hierarchy against these software titles to see which clients cannot run a certain application.

This information then becomes very useful when we are deploying a new operating system or a new application into our environment. It is a good validation step that can be used before deploying the software to give you a better idea of what will work and what will not work.

Licensing with asset intelligence

Another great feature of asset intelligence is to be able to import license statements. The most common use of this is to import your MVLS statement from the Microsoft VLSC. This will then allow you to look at reports, which show you how many licenses you have for a specific product and how many licenses you require if you are under licensed.

As well as importing the file provided by Microsoft, you can also create your own for third-party applications. This file is a specific format with headings, and more information about it can be found on TechNet. Adobe products are another common use for this; the majority of the organizations use this feature to validate their licensing for expensive products.

Controlling applications with the inventory data

It is not uncommon for organizations to provide applications based on roles. For example, users in finance may get one set of applications, and users within HR may get another set of applications.

Another scenario that is common is controlling installs and uninstalls via security groups in Active Directory. A lot has been written about the best way to populate collections. If a specific method fits your organization, then use it; you will end up with the same results.

Using security groups for application control

This method of controlling applications uses a combination of inventory and security groups in Active Directory. The basic principle behind this is as follows:

- Add the user to the Active Directory security group
- Collection members install based on a query looking for where the software is not installed and the user is a member of the security group
- Collection uninstalls based on a query looking for where the software is installed and the user is not a member of the security group

Using the application model in Configuration Manager makes this fairly easy to set up, as we use the same deployment type to specify the install and uninstall. For this example, create a security group in Active Directory, for example, Mozilla Firefox 22.

We will use two collections for this to work. One collection will be a query to determine which devices need the software (installation), and another will be used to determine which devices should have the software removed (uninstall).

Here is the query we will use for the installation collection; make sure you change the sections between the brackets highlighted:

```
select SMS_R_System.ResourceId, SMS_R_System.ResourceType, SMS_R_
System.Name, SMS_R_System.SMSUniqueIdentifier, SMS_R_System.
ResourceDomainORWorkgroup,
    SMS_R_System.Client
from  SMS_R_System inner join SMS_G_System_SYSTEM on SMS_G_System_
SYSTEM.ResourceID = SMS_R_System.ResourceId
where SMS_R_System.SystemGroupName = "<DomainName>\\<AD Group>" and
SMS_G_System_SYSTEM.Name not in
    (select SMS_R_System.Name from  SMS_R_System inner join SMS_G_
System_INSTALLED_SOFTWARE on
    SMS_G_System_INSTALLED_SOFTWARE.ResourceID = SMS_R_System.
ResourceId where SMS_G_System_INSTALLED_SOFTWARE.ARPDisplayName like
    "<AddRemoveProgramsDisplayName>")
```

In the following screenshot, you can also see an example of this in the graphical query designer:

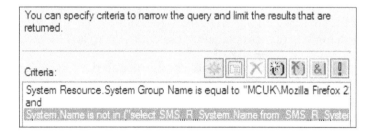

The uninstall collection is very similar. For this, we will need to use the following query. As you did earlier, make sure you modify the sections between the brackets that are highlighted:

```
select SMS_R_SYSTEM.ResourceID,SMS_R_SYSTEM.ResourceType,SMS_R_
SYSTEM.Name,SMS_R_SYSTEM.SMSUniqueIdentifier,SMS_R_SYSTEM.
ResourceDomainORWorkgroup,
    SMS_R_SYSTEM.Client
from  SMS_R_System inner join SMS_G_System_INSTALLED_SOFTWARE on
SMS_G_System_INSTALLED_SOFTWARE.ResourceID = SMS_R_System.ResourceId
```

```
    inner join SMS_G_System_SYSTEM on SMS_G_System_SYSTEM.ResourceID =
SMS_R_System.ResourceId
where SMS_G_System_INSTALLED_SOFTWARE.ARPDisplayName like
"<AddRemoveProgramsDisplayName>" and SMS_G_System_SYSTEM.Name not in

    (select SMS_R_System.Name from  SMS_R_System where SMS_R_System.
SystemGroupName = "<DomainName>\\<AD Group>")
```

As with the previous installation query, the following screenshot is how this will look in the query interface:

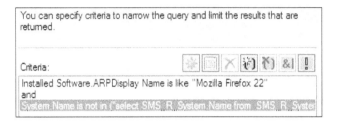

All that is left to do now is to create the deployment and select the appropriate action based on the collection you are deploying to. The collections will populate based on the membership of the group in Active Directory automatically.

Summary

In this chapter, we looked at some of the more common features in Configuration Manager that are usually just left not configured by most organizations. If they are configured, then it's usually the defaults. This chapter has shown how you can perform common management tasks using the data you collect in your inventory.

In the next chapter, we will look at how to configure and deploy System Center 2012 Endpoint Protection, and how you can configure your hierarchy to respond to threats to keep your environment safe.

4
Security with Endpoint Protection

One of the features of Configuration Manager that has had a big improvement in the System Center 2012 release is endpoint protection. In Configuration Manager 2007, we used **Forefront Endpoint Protection (FEP)** 2010. The integration to Configuration Manager was not the cleanest and was known for being quite a headache to manage.

Roll forward to Configuration Manager 2012, and **System Center 2012 Endpoint Protection (SCEP)** is a massive improvement in this space. In this chapter, we will look at SCEP 2012 in greater detail from an infrastructure perspective right through to updates and responding to threats. The topics we will cover in this chapter are as follows:

- Configuring the endpoint protection infrastructure
- Creating endpoint protection policies
- Deploying endpoint protection definition updates
- Deploying endpoint protection agents
- Controlling the Windows Firewall
- Responding to threats

Configuring the endpoint protection infrastructure

One of the biggest differences between FEP 2010 and SCEP 2012 is how much easier the core infrastructure is to set up. It is now lightning quick to deploy the additional role required for your primary site or central administration site.

The only prerequisite for the endpoint protection point role is that the software update point is also deployed, which is covered later in this chapter. The software update point is needed because this is used to obtain the latest definition updates for endpoint protection.

Your clients will then download and install the definition updates just like regular updates, and you can deploy them using automatic deployment rules.

Deploying the endpoint protection point

The endpoint protection point can be deployed in two ways and should be installed at the top of their hierarchy. The first way is using the traditional console method, where you can deploy other site system roles such as a distribution point, and the second way is using PowerShell.

Deploying the endpoint protection point with the console

In the administration workspace, expand **Site configuration** and click on the **Servers and Site System Roles** node. Right-click on the server you wish to deploy the role on and click on **Add Site System Roles**.

Click through to the **System Role Selection** screen, tick the endpoint protection point, and then click on **Next**. Agree to the license agreement and then configure your Microsoft Active Protection Service subscription preference.

Run through the rest of the wizard until you get to the **Summary** screen. Once you reach the **Summary** screen, click on **Next** to deploy the role to the server.

Deploying the endpoint protection point with PowerShell

As with most things in Configuration Manager, you can also deploy the endpoint protection point using a PowerShell command. From a Configuration Manager PowerShell window, you can enter the following command that will start the deployment and installation of the endpoint protection point:

```
Add-CMEndpointProtectionPoint -LicenseAgreed $True -ProtectionService
BasicMembership -SiteCode "CM1" -SiteSystemServerName "cm01.contoso.com"
```

Valid options for the `LicenseAgreed` parameter are either `true` or `false` (do not forget the dollar ($) sign). In order to proceed with the installation, you must specify `$true` here. The `ProtectionService` parameter allows you to determine what level of membership you would like in **Microsoft Active Protection Service (MAPS)**. You can enter `AdvancedMembership`, `BasicMembership`, or `DoNotJoinMaps` as valid options.

The other two parameters on this command line are the site code for your Configuration Manager site and the FQDN of the site system server where the role will be deployed.

About the Microsoft Active Protection Service

The MAPS, which was formally known as Microsoft SpyNet in previous versions of endpoint protection, is a community that includes users of SCEP. Joining the service automatically sends information back to Microsoft to help them determine which software is a potential threat and to help improve the effectiveness of SCEP.

Users who are opted into the program, even at the basic membership level, help stop the spread of new malware infections. If a report from MAPS includes details about malware that the endpoint protection client may be able to remove, MAPS will download the latest signature to address the infection. The same system also helps to identify false positives and fix them.

The basic membership level for MAPS means that reports sent to the Microsoft service contains telemetry about the potential infection. The following information can be included in this report:

- Filenames
- Cryptographic hash
- Vendor
- Size
- Date stamps

In addition to the preceding information, MAPS may contain the full URL to indicate the origin of the file. Users with the advanced subscription will see your reports containing the preceding information as well as the following information:

- Location of software
- How the software operates
- How it has impacted your system

Full information on how Microsoft uses this information can be found on the privacy statement for endpoint protection at `http://technet.microsoft.com/en-us/library/hh508835.aspx`.

 Subscribing to at least the basic telemetry can prevent your machines from experiencing zero day attacks, as information from other computers worldwide can help generate on-the-fly signatures before the definition ships in a scheduled update.

Creating endpoint protection policies

Creating endpoint protection policies is the essential part of endpoint protection and defines how endpoint protection works on client computers. As with client settings, a default policy is provided and any blanks that are not defined in overriding policies will be completed with sections of the default policy.

In the assets and compliance workspace under the endpoint protection node, you will find the node to manage endpoint protection policies. Additionally, as with client settings policies, endpoint protection policies are deployed on a per collection basis.

As with client settings, you can edit the default policy according to your requirements and create overrides and additions in other policies. Double-click on the policy to open the following policy window:

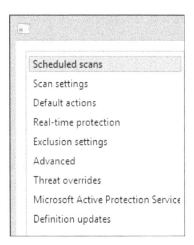

The options you can configure for endpoint protection are what you would expect from most antimalware solutions. As with all malware protection, it is really important to configure any vendor-recommended exclusions for products on your servers. The manufacturer will supply these and you can add them into your policy.

We will now create a workstation policy, which has custom scan settings from the defaults. Click on **Create Antimalware Policy**, enter a name for your policy, and then check the scan settings from the middle of the window. Just like client policy settings, you only configure the items that you check from the middle of the screen, as shown in the following screenshot:

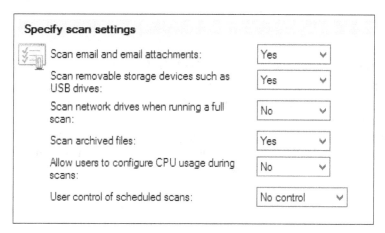

In the preceding screenshot, you can see that we have changed the values for e-mail and e-mail attachment scanning as well as scanning removable storage devices. As this policy is for workstation devices, it is a smart policy to enable on your devices as users will more than likely use e-mail on the device and may insert removable media.

When you have finished editing the settings you require and have added any additional settings, click on **OK** to create the policy. When you have finished with the policy and it has been created, you are now ready to deploy the policy.

Deploying endpoint protection policies

Deploying endpoint protection policies is a simple process; simply right-click on the policy that you wish to deploy and then select the collection on which you wish to deploy the collection to, as shown in the following screenshot:

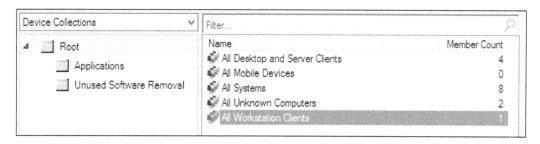

You can then click on the **Deployments** tab at the bottom of the console and see the collections that have an active deployment.

 Create your policies and deploy them before deploying the client. This way you have maximum protection before deploying your client.

Importing predefined policy templates

Included with the deployment of Configuration Manager is a number of predefined templates, which include customized scan settings for specific Microsoft products. You can find these templates at <drive>\Program Files\Microsoft Configuration Manager\AdminConsole\XmlStorage\EPTemplates. These can be imported as a good base for your policy; you can then make any modifications you require for your environment on top before saving the policy, as shown in the following screenshot:

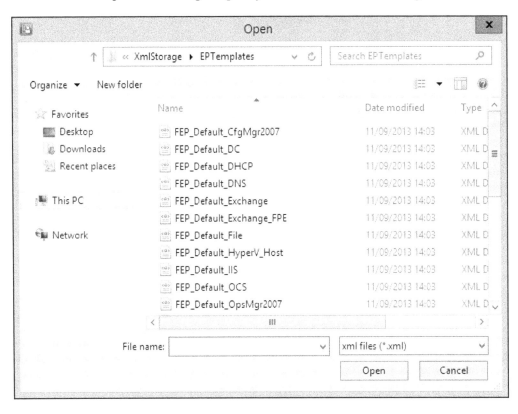

In the following screenshot, you can see the exclusions in a standard server policy, which is a template from the list in the preceding screenshot:

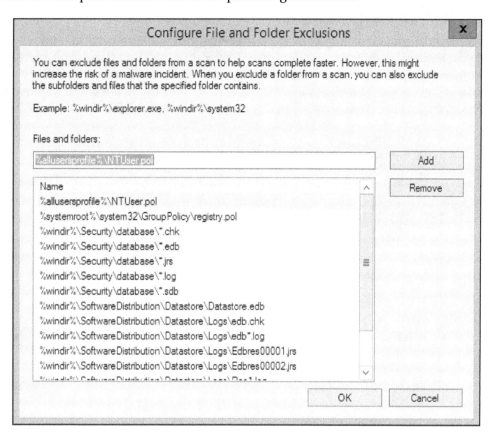

You can see that Microsoft has provided the recommended exclusions for this policy.

Imported policies are no different from the policies that you create yourself. They can be edited, merged, and deployed in the exact same way. Policy templates exist for products, such as Hyper-V, Exchange, IIS, SQL Server, and many more.

 For Microsoft products, use the predefined templates that include the recommended extensions.

Deploying endpoint protection definition updates

To successfully and efficiently protect your clients, you will also need to deploy the latest definition updates to your clients. Endpoint protection client definitions are similar to signature updates in other antivirus products. They are available via **Windows Server Updates Services (WSUS)** and can be downloaded and deployed using Configuration Manager.

In order to deploy the definition updates, you first need a software update point. This is actually a prerequisite for setting up the endpoint protection point anyway, so it should already be in place.

Setting up the software update point

Configuration Manager supports the deployment of definition updates just like any other update. They are treated the same as a regular security update for Windows or a critical update for Internet Explorer.

Ensure that in your software update point, component settings under the **Sites** node in the **Administration** workspace has the category **Definition Updates** and the product **Forefront Endpoint Protection 2010** selected. The following screenshot shows you how this configuration should look:

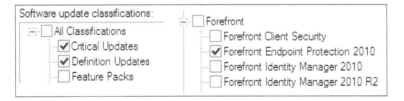

Once you have completed this configuration, the software update point is set up, and you are now ready to begin deploying definition updates to your endpoint protection clients.

The definitions available for Forefront Endpoint Protection 2010 are also the ones used in System Center Endpoint Protection 2012, so this is why **Forefront** is selected in the products list.

Using automatic deployment rules

The easiest way to deploy your definition updates is by using the automatic deployment rules, which are in the software updates functionality of Configuration Manager. This function allows you to set up a rule to look for updates, execute the rule on a schedule, and then deploy the updates found by the rule.

To make the deployment of definition updates even easier, Microsoft has provided a template for the automatic deployment rule:

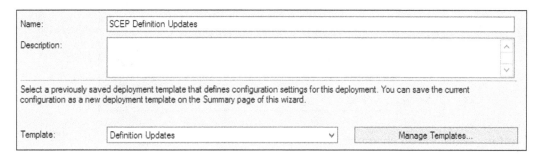

As you can see in the preceding screenshot, you need to give your automatic deployment rule a name. This should be something descriptive that you can easily relate to if you need to modify the settings again in the future.

From the template drop-down box, you can then select **Definition Updates**. This will complete the rest of the wizard with some predefined settings, which are recommended by Microsoft. Let's walk through these settings, verify them, and make any changes we might want to make.

Before you click on **Next**, select the collection you wish to deploy the updates to. Note that this must be a device collection. Leave all the other settings on this screen as default and then click on **Next**. Accept all the defaults on the **Deployment Settings** screen as well and click on **Next**.

On the **Software Updates** screen, you can see that the wizard has already selected the correct product and update classification for us. This is because we selected the definition updates template in the first step.

In the bottom-right corner of the same screen, you will see a **Preview** button; click on this to test out your criteria. If your software update point has performed synchronization since you added the product and classification for synchronization, then you should see some definition updates, as shown in the following screenshot:

			Preview updates
Configuration Manager returned 6 updates.			
Filter...			
Title	Article ID	Bulletin ID	Product
Definition Update for Micr...	2461484		"Forefront Endpoint Protection 2010"
Definition Update for Micr...	2461484		"Forefront Endpoint Protection 2010"
Definition Update for Micr...	2461484		"Forefront Endpoint Protection 2010"
Definition Update for Micr...	2461484		"Forefront Endpoint Protection 2010"
Definition Update for Micr...	2461484		"Forefront Endpoint Protection 2010"
Definition Update for Micr...	2461484		"Forefront Endpoint Protection 2010"

Nothing should need changing on this page so just click on **Next**.

 Use the **Preview** button to ensure that you are picking up the correct updates before creating the rule. It is always worth double-checking the results.

On the **Evaluation Schedule** screen, we can set the settings that determine when the rule will be executed on the site. Using the template, the default should be fine; this should state to execute the rule after the software update point has completed its synchronization as definitions can be released three times a day. This setting works great as it means we are only ever going to execute the rule following the completion of a synchronization run. This also ensures that each time the rule is executed the latest definition updates will be deployed; when you are happy with this setting, click on **Next**.

On the **Deployment Schedule** screen, the default settings are provided for you, which are usually good enough; however, if you manage devices over multiple time zones, then you may want to look at this screen more carefully.

First of all, we have the option to specify how the schedule will be evaluated. The options for this setting are **Universal Coordinated Time (UTC)** or the local time of the client. UTC is the default setting; however, if you manage many clients over many time zones, then you might want to consider changing this setting.

For example, if the rule was set up to execute at 12:00 hours every day, and we then said make the updates available one hour after the rule has run, then every client, regardless of the time zone, would run at 13:00.

For definition updates, this setting is generally ignored as we want our clients to update as quickly as possible as the definition updates could contain important detection for a zero-day attack.

 To deploy your definition updates as quickly as possible, accept the defaults on the **Deployment Schedule** screen of the wizard.

On the **User Experience** screen, by default, the wizard allows software installation outside of a maintenance window when the deadline is reached. As a recommendation, uncheck this option so that you know that even in maintenance windows you are only deploying definition updates.

Ensure your settings match the ones shown in the following screenshot, unless you have specific requirements that dictate otherwise:

User visual experience
User notifications: Hide in Software Center and all notifications

Deadline behavior

When the installation deadline is reached, allow the following activities to be performed outside o

☐ Software Installation
☐ System restart (if necessary)

Device restart behavior

Some software updates require a system restart to complete the installation process. You can s workstations.

Suppress the system restart on the following devices:

☐ Servers
☐ Workstations

Write filter handling for Windows Embedded devices
☐ Commit changes at deadline or during a maintenance window (requires restarts)
If this option is not selected, content will be applied on the overlay and committed later.

Click on **Next** to go to the **Alerts** screen. In any environment security, updates are important and it is important to know when we fall below a percentage of compliance in our environment. Definition updates are as important as security updates, and Configuration Manager through the automatic deployment rules wizard provides us with the ability to generate alerts if our compliance percentage falls.

Check the top box, which is labeled **Generate an alert when the following conditions are met**; when you check the box, the default percentage is 90. The highest you can go is 99, however, this would not be recommended as it would be very difficult to attain that high-compliance percentage.

 The value for this setting should be discussed with your security team as they will likely have an input of what they would like to see.

For definition updates, we do not set a deadline; however, if you have decided to set a deadline, then you can choose to generate the alert after a set amount of time has passed since the end of the deadline. This provides your clients with time to update before the alert is thrown. If you do not specify a deadline, then this is simply ignored.

If you are running Operations Manager and your target devices are monitored with the Operations Manager agent, then you also have the option to suspend alerting during updates. This can be useful if the updates restart a monitored service for example. This will prevent generating updates needlessly. If the update fails, you can also generate an Operations Manager alert.

The following screenshot shows the recommended configuration to alert the definition updates:

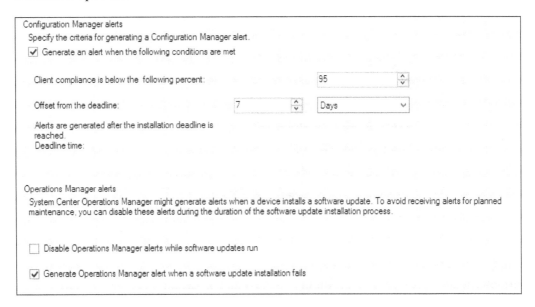

As per the preceding screenshot, only check the **Generate Operations Manager alert when a software update installation fails** option if you are running Operations Manager.

 For integration with an existing Operations Manager environment for alerting, utilize the options available in the wizard.

Accept the rest of the default settings until you get to the **Deployment Package** screen. If you are running the wizard for the first time, create a new deployment package, and provide the name of the package along with the **Uniform Naming Convention** (**UNC**) path to the directory where you want to keep the content before it is deployed.

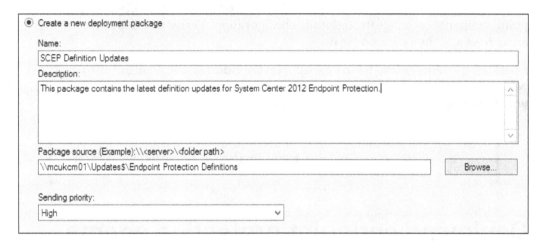

As with other parts of the console, always make sure your names are meaningful not only to yourself later down the line but to your colleagues as well who also use the console. Also, provide a description so others can see what the deployment package is for and what it contains. Looking at the description is much easier and quicker than finding the automatic deployment rule again to see which package is used.

Leave the **Sending priority** option as **High**. This is important as it will make sure that if other deployments are currently ongoing, the sender will drop lower priority content in order to make sure the content is deployed quickly.

 Set the **Sending priority** option **Too high** to make sure content is deployed as quickly as possible.

Click on **Next** to define which distribution points or distribution point groups you would like the content on and then select where the updates will come from. This is most likely the Internet but depending on your configuration it could also be another UNC path.

The language choices that are preselected are the ones from the software update point component settings from the site configuration. Verify whether these settings are correct and then click on **Next**.

Check all the settings you have provided on the **Summary** screen and then click on **Next** to create the automatic deployment rule. As we are using the template, the rule will be enabled by default and will run at the next defined schedule.

 You should make sure that the software update point has finished synchronizing and then manually start the automatic deployment rule for the first time.

Deploying endpoint protection agents

Once your policies have been set up and you have configured the automatic deployment of definition updates, the next step is to deploy the endpoint protection agent. The agent can be deployed in numerous ways. In this section, we will look at deploying the agent by configuring the settings in client policies and also deploying the agent in task sequences during operating system deployment.

Deploying agents using client settings policies

If you are enabling a global deployment of endpoint protection, then the following changes can be made to the default policy or your own default policy, if you have one. If you only plan to deploy endpoint protection to a subset of machines for testing for example, then create a new policy that only configures those settings we will configure and deploy that policy to your test collection.

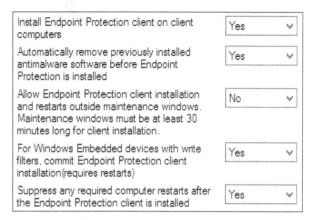

As you can see from the preceding screenshot, not many settings need changing. You can find all of these settings under the endpoint protection category in your client settings. Setting the first option to **Yes** instructs the agent to begin the deployment of the endpoint protection agent.

The second setting specifies if other antimalware products should be removed before the endpoint protection agent is installed. It is common for multiple antimalware products on the same machine to cause problems. Configuration Manager supports the removal of the following products:

- Symantec AntiVirus Corporate Edition v10
- Symantec Endpoint Protection v11
- Symantec Endpoint Protection Small Business Edition v12
- McAfee VirusScan Enterprise v8
- Trend Micro OfficeScan
- Microsoft Forefront Codename Stirling Beta 2
- Microsoft Forefront Codename Stirling Beta 3
- Microsoft Forefront Client Security v1
- Microsoft Security Essentials v1

- Microsoft Security Essentials 2010
- Microsoft Forefront Endpoint Protection 2010
- Microsoft Security Center Online v1

Where your product is not listed, you can use the software distribution functionality of Configuration Manager to remove your product and then deploy endpoint protection. The third option suppresses the reboot of computers outside of the maintenance windows. The fourth option is for devices that run an embedded version of Windows; in this case, the changes made to the system during the installation of the agent will be committed and saved.

The final option is a security net and will prevent any devices from restarting following the installation of endpoint protection. This is highly recommended for all devices, servers, and workstations alike.

Deploying endpoint protection in your image

You can also deploy the endpoint protection agent in your old image. This can be done by deploying the agent as normal, before you sysprep the agent. The following registry keys contain unique information about the agent and must be deleted. All the keys can be found in `HKEY_LOCAL_MACHINE`.

- `SOFTWARE\Microsoft\Microsoft Antimalware\InstallTime`
- `SOFTWARE\Microsoft\Microsoft Antimalware\Scan\LastScanRun`
- `SOFTWARE\Microsoft\Microsoft Antimalware\Scan\LastScanType`
- `SOFTWARE\Microsoft\Microsoft Antimalware\Scan\LastQuickScanID`
- `SOFTWARE\Microsoft\Microsoft Antimalware\Scan\LastFullScanID`
- `SOFTWARE\Microsoft\RemovalTools\MRT\GUID`

Once these keys have been deleted, you can then complete the sysprep process including capturing your image. You can script this, so this step doesn't need to be manual.

Responding to threats

Keeping a secure environment is a two-fold job; keeping the agents updated with the latest definitions is one thing but what about when the protection fails for some reason? How do we respond to these threats?

For collections, you can right-click on them in the **Assets and Compliance** workspace and manually run a quick scan, full scan, or a manual definition update.

Monitoring endpoint protection

It is important to monitor the status of your endpoint protection. As with most things in Configuration Manager, monitoring is done per collection. Right-click on a collection and select **Properties**. Click on the **Alerts** tab of the collection properties, and check the box **View this collection in the Endpoint Protection dashboard**. Then, click on the **Add** button to add the alerts you want to monitor at this specific collection. Add all of the alerts related to endpoint protection. Let's have a look at the options for each alert.

The first alert **Malware detection** is a simple alert, which alerts you when any malware is found on any member of the collection. A default name is generated for you; you can change this if you wish to something a little shorter or more customized. Set the severity of the alert; the default is **Critical** and it is suggested you keep this as **Critical**. The final option on this alert is to set the threshold to either **High**, **Medium**, or **Low**.

The second alert, **Malware outbreak,** allows us to throw an alert based on the percentage of clients that have detected malware. The default says to throw a critical alert when one percent of the clients have detected malware.

The final two, as shown in the following screenshot, **Repeated malware detection** and **Multiple malware detection** are very similar. They only differ in the number of times malware was detected or the types of malware detected.

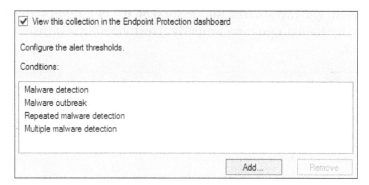

When you have configured your alert settings, your collection properties should look like the preceding screenshot. When you have applied the settings, go to the **Monitoring** workspace and expand the **Endpoint Protection Status** node; here, click on the first node. If you have multiple collections, you will be able to select them from the dropdown at the top of the screen.

The reporting will show you multiple bits of information at a glance. The following screenshot shows you information on the security state, which is clients with active protection, clients classed as at risk, and the malware remediation status.

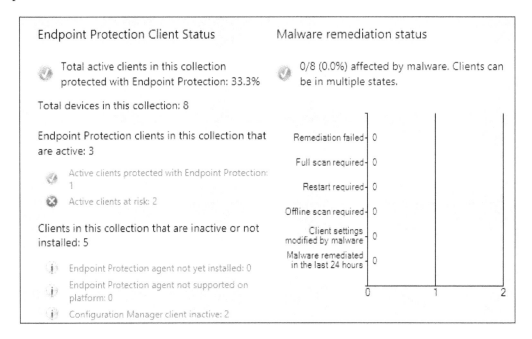

In the same screen, you can also see information on the definition status of clients, such as how many are not updating properly. The following screenshot shows this information:

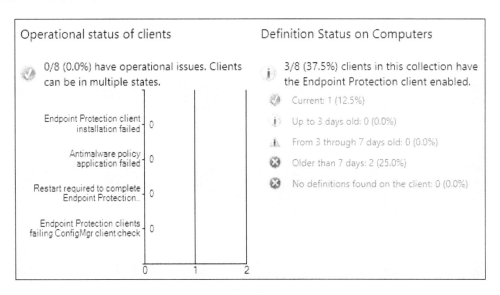

Each section by the side of a graph and the blue links are clickable to show you more information and a list of machines that fall into the category you have clicked. Configuration Manager also contains a number of built-in reports, which you can see in the **Reports** node in the **Monitoring** workspace.

The following screenshot shows you the reports that are available out of the box with Configuration Manager:

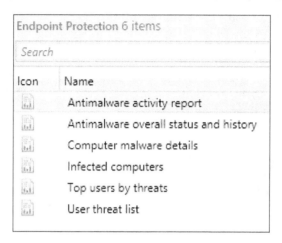

Managing threat alerts

Alerts that are set on a collection are viewed and triggered just like any other alert, such as the alert for management point health. Additionally, like other alerts, you can also create subscriptions to these alerts so they can be e-mailed out.

In the preceding screenshot, you can see we have created an alert that will send alerts to our security team's mailbox; this will alert them to potential problems without giving them access to the console. We can also give them access to the reports without the console.

Testing endpoint protection with EICAR

In order to test your endpoint protection configuration and notification, you can perform a simple test of the functionality using EICAR, a test virus signature that is available for free at `http://bit.ly/1qNP0WM`.

EICAR can be used as a safe way to test your configuration of endpoint protection and test your security to ensure that you are properly protected. Endpoint protection contains protection for the test signature.

Controlling the Windows Firewall

Configuration Manager contains a method to allow the simple control of your Windows Firewall settings. By simple, we mean having the ability to perform the following configuration:

- Control if the firewall is on or off
- Control if incoming connections are blocked
- Control if users are notified when a program is blocked

If you want to control the rules on the firewall, then this configuration still needs to be done in group policy rather than Configuration Manager as this configuration is not currently possible.

What this configuration does allow is the ability to control the Windows Firewall on nondomain-joined resources.

Summary

In this chapter, we looked at how to deploy and manage System Center 2012 Endpoint Protection end to end. We looked at how to configure the infrastructure, create and manage polices, deploy definition updates, deploy agents, and manage alerts and respond to malware threats.

In the next chapter, we will look at content management within Configuration Manager; we will look at how to deploy cloud-based distribution points, understand how content flows to distribution points, and how caching solutions can be used to manage content flow.

5
Advanced Content Management

Another big change in Configuration Manager is the introduction of the content library. The content library is used to store content on your distribution points for applications, packages, driver packages, software update packages, and much more. This introduction enables smarter management of the space required to store your content and includes the use of single instance storage.

In order to reduce the number of secondary sites required in Configuration Manager over the previous versions, the distribution point now uses a sender. This would have been only on secondary sites in the previous versions.

Cloud computing has also changed the way organizations work recently. Configuration Manager also contains functionality to create distribution points, which are in Windows Azure. We will cover the following topics in this chapter:

- How to deploy distribution points
- How to deploy cloud distribution points
- Understanding the content library
- Introducing network caching
- Working with deduplication

Deploying distribution points

A major strength of Configuration Manager is the fact that it is a highly flexible and customizable application. This means that when we distribute any content using Configuration Manager, providing the setup is correct, then it should have no negative impact on the **wide area network (WAN)** in any way.

The placement of distribution points is something that requires careful consideration and should be planned carefully. Information on your network such as an overview of the topology of your network as well as utilization information for your network links is also critical information, which will help you plan the placement and configuration of distribution points in your environment.

Planning for the placement of distribution points

As a typical scenario, imagine an environment with nine remote sites. The headquarters site is also where the primary site is deployed. We will simply refer to these sites as the following cities:

- London
- Edinburgh
- New York
- Cape Town
- Sydney
- Brisbane
- Toronto
- Beijing
- Auckland

The sites at London, Edinburgh, New York, Cape Town, and Sydney are running with very good links to the primary site, whereas the sites at Brisbane, Toronto, Beijing, and Auckland are running over slower links to the primary site. Of the sites with good links, Cape Town and Sydney have users that run applications requiring a high amount of bandwidth during business hours which are 8 a.m. till 5 p.m. During this time, we should restrict traffic to these distribution points.

The sites at Brisbane, Toronto, and Beijing contain employees that control critical systems overnight. For these sites, transfers should be restricted to daytime hours only so that content is not distributed overnight. While Auckland is a slow link to the primary site, the link to Brisbane is fast, so this should be taken into consideration as well.

Of the remaining sites, London, Edinburgh, and New York have no additional configurations that should be considered.

Now that we have all the information, we need to decide on the placement of the distribution points and any configuration that needs to be implemented.

Placement of distribution points with fast connectivity

As we have already established, London, Edinburgh, New York, Cape Town, and Sydney are running off fast links. We have no special considerations to make for sites one to three, so these can be standard distribution points with no additional configuration or no distribution points at all.

While Cape Town and Sydney also have good connectivity, we need to limit the bandwidth that can be used between the hours of 8 a.m. and 5 p.m. As these are the business hours for these locations, traffic will be allowed; however, the following limitations will be placed on the configuration of the distribution point:

- Between the hours of 8 a.m. and 5 p.m., only high priority transfers will be allowed

- Transfer rates will be limited to 25 percent of the available bandwidth between the hours of 8 a.m. and 5 p.m.

Configuration Manager only knows about the bandwidth available to it on the WAN, for example, traffic management or quality of service may dictate 1 Mbps of bandwidth. Configuration Manager will allow us to use a percentage of this limit.

Placement of distribution points with slow connectivity

We have already established that sites six to nine are running as slow links. These require more configuration and additional thought on the placement of these systems to ensure that Configuration Manager is working to its maximum ability.

We need to place special configuration on Brisbane, Toronto, and Beijing. The following restrictions will be placed on these distribution points. These settings are configured on the properties of the distribution point in the sites and site system server's node in the **Administration** workspace.

- Between the hours of 5 p.m. and 8 a.m., transfers will be closed to all priorities
- Between 8 a.m. and 5 p.m., transfers are limited to sending 400 KB pulses of data every 60 seconds

Auckland is a special case. We have already established that the connectivity to the primary site is very poor, and that connectivity to site six is much faster. The connection for site nine is not as fast as sites one to five though. For this site, the following configuration will be required:

- Distribution point at this site will be configured to pull content from the distribution point at Brisbane
- Between 8 a.m. and 5 p.m., transfers will be limited to 50 percent of the available bandwidth

Creating distribution points using the console

Distribution points that are not deployed on a site system such as a primary site or secondary site are known as remote site systems. In the **Administration** workspace in the console, go to the **Servers and site system roles** node within the Site configuration folder.

From here, click on **Create Site System Server** from the ribbon or right-click on the **Console** node and select the same option. When the wizard opens, click on the **Browse** button and find the server where you want to deploy the distribution point. Select the site code that you want to attach the distribution point to. The following screenshot is the sample configuration that you would potentially use to deploy a distribution point to a server that is in a trusted forest:

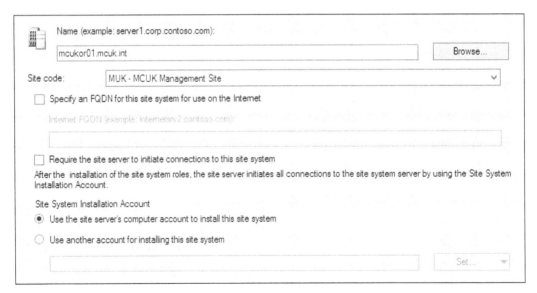

You can use a specific installation account rather than the computer account of the site server. Either way, ensure that the computer account or the domain account you specify is a local administrator on the target system.

If the target is on an untrusted domain, then make sure that the checkbox **Require the site server to initiate connections** to this site system is checked and also that the installation account you specify is an account in the untrusted forest and it has local administration rights on the target server.

Click on **Next** to go through to the **System Role Selection** screen; check the **Distribution point** option and then click on **Next**.

A distribution point contains source files for clients to download.

☑ Install and configure IIS if required by Configuration Manager

☐ Enable and configure BranchCache for this distribution point

Description: Site One Distribution Point

Specify how client computers communicate with this distribution point.

⦿ HTTP

Does not support mobile devices or Mac computers.

○ HTTPS

Requires computers to have a valid PKI client certificate:

Allow intranet-only connections

If you manage Mac computers or have mobile devices that are enrolled by Configuration Manager, select an option that allows Internet client connections.

☐ Allow clients to connect anonymously

Check the **Install and configure IIS if required by Configuration Manager** box if you haven't already installed the requirements to this server. Give a description as well; this will be visible when deploying content, so will enable people to identify a distribution point without knowing the name of the server.

Once you have configured the settings you require, click on **Next** to continue. We can also use the skpswi.dat file to prevent the inventory of files in a specific directory and no_sms_on_drive.sms to prevent site components from installing on a specific drive.

Primary content library location:	D:
Secondary content library location:	Automatic
Primary package share location:	D:
Secondary package share location:	Automatic

On the drive settings screen, select the drive you want as the primary location for the content library and package share. This will be the default location where Configuration Manager will deploy the content library and package share used to store content deployed to this distribution point.

Setting the secondary location to automatic, which is the default, means that Configuration Manager will automatically determine the best place to put the content library and package share, should it be required. Automatic means the drive with the maximum space will be used. When you are happy with the settings provided here, click on **Next**.

If you require support for PXE boot, then check the box on the **PXE Settings** screen and configure any additional settings that you might require, as shown in the following screenshot:

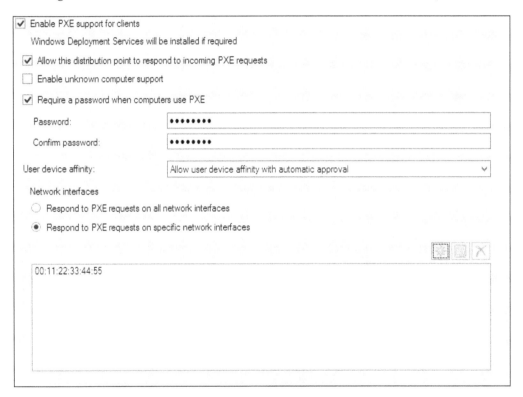

In the preceding screenshot, you can see we have configured a PXE support for this distribution point. This will be used for the operating system deployment and will automatically install the **Windows Deployment Services (WDS)** role if required.

We have also checked the box to enable the distribution point to respond to incoming requests and enabled a password for computers. User device affinity has also been configured, which will enable devices to automatically allow affinity.

The final setting we have set on this screen allows us to configure the PXE role to only respond to requests on a network interface that match the specific network adapter. This can be very useful if the target server has multiple network adapters and one of those adapters has specific network configuration for a build network, for example. Click on **Next** to configure the multicast settings.

Multicast is a network optimization method that you can use when multiple clients are likely to download the same operating system image at the same time. When multicast is used, multiple computers simultaneously download the operating system image as it is multicast by the distribution point, rather than having the distribution point send a copy of the data to each client over a separate connection.

 Multicast may not speed up your operating system deployments but will optimize the network to deliver the image.

The content validation process verifies the integrity of content files on distribution points. When the content validation process starts, Configuration Manager verifies the content files on distribution points, and if the file hash is unexpected for the files on the distribution point, Configuration Manager creates a status message that you can review in the monitoring workspace.

On the final configuration screen of the wizard, you can add the distribution point to a boundary group. In the previous versions of Configuration Manager, this configuration would be the same as making the distribution point a protected site system to a specific boundary.

Creating distribution points using PowerShell

You can use the Configuration Manager PowerShell command shell to also deploy a distribution point. The following PowerShell command will deploy a distribution point with the following settings:

- The server name is set to cmdp01.contoso.com
- The site code is set to C01
- Install and configure IIS if required
- The minimum disk space is set to 50 MB
- The primary location and share is set to D

- The secondary location and share is set to `Automatic`:

```
Add-CMDistributionPoint -SiteSystemServerName "cmdp01.contoso.
com" -SiteCode "C01" -InstallInternetServer -ClientConnectionType
Intranet CertificateExpirationTimeUTC "2100/01/01 00:00:00"
-MinimumFreeSpaceMB 50 -PrimaryContentLibraryLocation D
-SecondaryContentLibraryLocation Automatic -PrimaryShare D
-SecondaryShare Automatic
```

When this command runs, the distribution point is deployed. You can use the usual methods such as the component status monitoring and log files to see the deployment and installation of the distribution point. The process is no different, just arguably quicker using PowerShell.

How to deploy cloud distribution points

As computing enters a new era and we see a big shift towards the cloud, Configuration Manager has also embraced this. We have the ability to deploy cloud-based distribution points that utilize the Windows Azure infrastructure.

 You must have a Windows Azure subscription for this to work, which will incur additional costs. Make sure you know how much you are spending.

Cloud distribution points are easy to set up, easy to deploy and manage, as well as cost effective. You can easily price up the cost of a cloud distribution point using the price calculator on the Windows Azure website.

 Large content is not suitable for Windows Azure, such as content used in the operating system deployment.

The best thing is that you can start and stop them at will making them a valuable tool for various uses:

- A need to rapidly deploy software
- Serve content on the Internet without exposing a server
- Serve content for VPN users
- Clients can fallback if a local or remote distribution point does not have the content

 If you are deploying on a budget, then consider cloud distribution points. They can be more cost effective for shorter periods than provisioning a server.

How the service works

Within your Windows Azure subscription, Configuration Manager creates some blob storage to store your applications and packages. A cloud service is also created, and this is what the Configuration Manager client will attempt to connect to in order to retrieve content.

You can treat cloud distribution points exactly like on premise distribution points. In this, you can add them to distribution point groups. The way you distribute the content to both is the same process and the integration with the console is such that you can treat them just like a part of your management infrastructure.

A number of caveats exist when considering the use of cloud distribution points. These should be considered before you use them:

- Uploads to Windows Azure are free but data leaving your account is charged
- Software updates are not supported, and neither are updates created in System Center Update Publisher
- Clients will always try to find content elsewhere first and fallback to the cloud distribution point as a last resort
- BranchCache is automatically configured on the cloud distribution point, so if you can configure this on your clients, then you should

Creating the management certificate

Windows Azure requires the machines that connect to it to provision services in the cloud, which must have a management certificate. This is the authentication mechanism that Windows Azure will use to certify that the calling server or workstation is allowed to provision services in the subscription.

If your hierarchy contains a central administration site, then the certificate we need should be requested on the primary site. Just like a regular distribution point, the cloud distribution point will be attached to the primary site and not the central administration site.

Creating the certificate template

Using an internal certification authority such as Active Directory Certificate Services is an easy way to provision the certificate that is required for Windows Azure. As with other types of certificates, a template is recommended to ensure the certificate that is requested by the endpoint is the correct one for the purpose it was intended.

1. Open the **Certification Authority** management console from **Administrative Tools** or from the **Tools** menu in **Server Manager**.

2. Right-click on **Certificate Templates** in the console and then click on **Manage**.

3. In the templates window, find the web server template, right-click on the template, and select **Duplicate Template**.

4. Enter a descriptive name for the template such as `Windows Azure Management Certificate` on the **General** tab, as shown in the following screenshot:

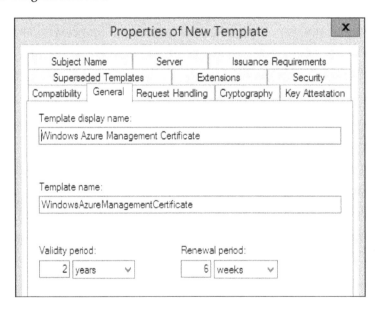

This works well because the template can be used to provision the management certificate on any system that requires access to your Windows Azure subscription, not just Configuration Manager.

On the **Request Handling** tab, make sure that **Allow private key to be exported** is checked. This is very important as we will be exporting the certificate with the private key in.

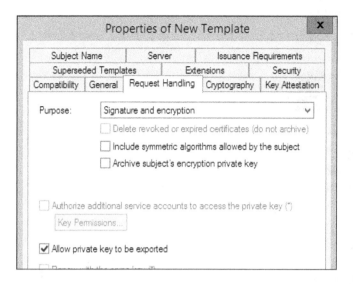

Finally, on the **Security** tab, as a recommendation, create a security group in Active Directory, and add the group into the **Security** window. Make sure that the newly added object has **Read** and **Enroll** permissions on the template:

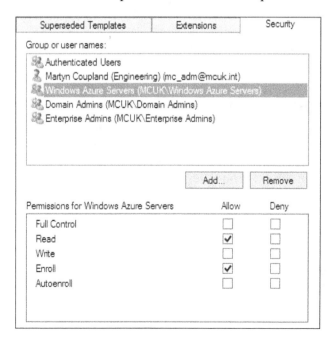

Click on **OK** and then close the **Certificate Templates** console. Again, right-click on **Certificate Templates** and select **New Certificate Template to Issue**. Select the certificate that you have just created and then click on **OK**, as shown in the following screenshot:

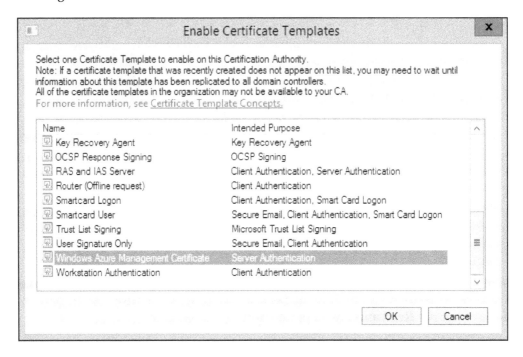

As the certificate template has now been provisioned, we must now provision the certificate on the primary site.

How to enroll the certificate

On the primary site server, open a new **Microsoft Management Console** (**MMC**) and add the certificates snap-in. Make sure that the console is set to view the local computer. Open the **Personal** certificate store, right-click on **Certificates** and select **Request New Certificate**, as shown in the following screenshot:

Click through to the enrolment policy and select **Active Directory Enrollment Policy**. On the **Request Certificates** page, select the template you have created, then click on the link that says **More information is required to enroll for this certificate**.

At this point, you need to decide what you want your distribution point to be called. It must be a **fully qualified domain name (FQDN)** and should not already exist in DNS. Also, ensure that you use the correct FQDN if your organization has one domain for internal use and one for external.

In **Subject name**, select **Common name** in the **Type** drop-down box and type in the name of the distribution point, for example, `cdp01.contoso.com` or `cdp01.internal.contoso.com`. Additionally, in the **Alternative name** section, change the **Type** drop-down box to **DNS** and type the same value you used earlier, as shown in the following screenshot:

Click on **OK** and then press **Enroll** to complete the enrollment of the certificate.

Exporting the management certificate

When the certificate has been enrolled, it must be exported in two formats: one without the private key, which will be a CER file extension, and another that will contain the private key and is a PFX file extension.

In the certificates snap-in connected to the local computer, right-click on the certificate from the personal certificate store, select **All Tasks**, and then click on **Export**. On the first page, click on **Next**. Select **No, do not export the private key**, and then click on **Next** again, as shown in the following screenshot:

On the **Export Format** screen, ensure that **DER encoded binary X.509 (.CER)** is selected, click on **Next**, and save the resulting file.

Now that you have exported the certificate file, we now need the private key file. Right-click on the certificate again and select **All Tasks** and **Export** again. This time, select **Yes, I want to export the private key** and then export the certificate with the rest of the default settings, as shown in the following screenshot:

Add a password to the file, as shown in the following screenshot, for security, so you can only use the PFX file if you know the password on the exported certificate:

Uploading the management certificate to Windows Azure

Log in to the Windows Azure Management Portal (`http://manage.windowsazure.com`), once you are logged in, go to **Settings** on the bottom-left corner of the window; you might have to scroll in the grey side bar.

Click on **Management Certificates** and then on **Upload** at the bottom of the screen. Upload the CER file that you saved to upload the certificate to Windows Azure.

Once the certificate has been uploaded, you will see the confirmation at the bottom of the screen. Before you close or log out of the portal, you will need the subscription ID of your subscription for Configuration Manager. When your certificate has uploaded, you can find this next to the certificate name, just as you can see in the following screenshot:

Creating the cloud distribution point

In the **Administration** workspace in the **Configuration Manager** console, expand **Cloud Services** and right-click on the **Cloud Distribution Points** node and select **Create Cloud Distribution Point**.

Enter the subscription ID of the subscription in Windows Azure where you want to create the cloud distribution point and browse to the path of the PFX file; enter the password that you put on the file when prompted.

When you click on **Next**, Configuration Manager will connect to Windows Azure and verify the information you have provided. This might take a minute or two. On the **Settings** screen, make a note of the service name that appears as this will be required shortly. Provide a description of the cloud distribution point and specify the default region where the data will be stored.

You will also need to provide the primary site where the cloud distribution point will be installed and again enter the PFX file and password. Click on **Next** and configure the expected storage and bandwidth requirements for this cloud distribution point to allow an alert; this is highly recommended.

Finish the wizard and the cloud distribution point will be created. This can take around 30 minutes to complete, once the service has been provisioned. The console will report the status as **Ready**.

 Configure limits as this will prevent unnecessary charges and allow you to keep an eye on the usage of the service.

The cloud distribution point is now ready, and you can deploy content to it in the same way you would normal distribution points.

Creating the DNS entry

For your clients to resolve the name you have provided in the certificate, take the service name from the setup name and create a CNAME entry in DNS that points your entry to the service name followed by `<servicename>.cloudapp.net`.

Allowing clients to use cloud distribution points

Before your clients can communicate with any cloud distribution points that you have made, you will need to either edit the default client settings or create a custom client settings policy to allow the use of cloud distribution points.

If you are trailing the functionality as a recommendation, create a new custom policy which only has this setting in.

Understanding the content library

In the world of content distribution within Configuration Manager, the introduction of the content library is the biggest change. The content library will efficiently store content, which you will distribute to your distribution points. Single instance storage is also used on the content share. If the same package, for example, uses the same content, only one instance will be stored and references kept to indicate the file will be part of both the packages.

The whole reason for the introduction of the content library is to optimize storage space and avoid the distribution of files, which already exist on the distribution point in order to save bandwidth usage on WAN. Single instance storage will even work if the files are named differently. This is a common misconception that the file has to be named the same to be single instance stored.

Anatomy of the content library

The content library is stored in the root of a drive in a folder called SCCMContentLib. To prevent accidental damage, permissions are set when the folder is shared out. This is done when the distribution point role is installed.

Within the root of the folder, you will see the following three folders:

- Package library (PkgLib)
- Data library (DataLib)
- File library (FileLib)

The package library contains information about the packages that are distributed to the specific distribution point. The data library contains information about the structure of the package and finally the file library contains the original files in the package. Typically, this is where you will see most of the storage space used.

In the following diagram, you can see an example of how everything fits together in the content library. The following diagram illustrates the relationship between the three folders and how the content might look:

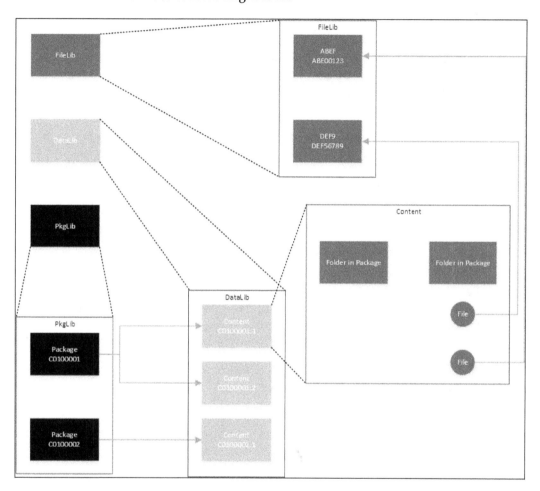

Package library

In the previous versions of Configuration Manager, you would have been able to just browse the package share and look at the content stored in the specific package ID folders. With the new content library this is not possible; however, you can use the Content Library Explorer, which is discussed in more detail in *Chapter 12, Advanced Troubleshooting*.

In order to use the run from distribution point functionality, Configuration Manager requires packages existing on the share as per the previous versions, where the drive letter is used on the SMSPKG share.

Let's start in the `PkgLib` folder. In this folder, you will see a file for each package that is stored on the distribution point. The filename will be the package ID and the format of the file is an INI file.

Under the packages section of the file (this will apply to any that you open in the `PkgLib` folder), you will see a list of content ID numbers as well as other information about the package such as the content version.

With the content ID, we can start browsing the rest of the library and use the version to determine the version of the content. In the following screenshot, our content ID is `MUK00007.1`:

Data library

Now that we have determined the content ID of the package, we can use this information to browse the rest of the library. In the data library or DataLib, we will find one folder and one file for each of the contents within a package. For example, you will see MUK00007.1 and MUK00007.1.INI. The file will contain information that is used for validation and inside the folder, the structure from the original package is recreated.

Files that make up the content of the package will be replaced in the data library, though, with INI files. This file contains information about the file such as the modification timestamp, hash of the file, and the size of the file. Using the hash, we then continue browsing the library to be able to find the original file. For this, we need the first four characters of the hash 192D as highlighted in the following screenshot:

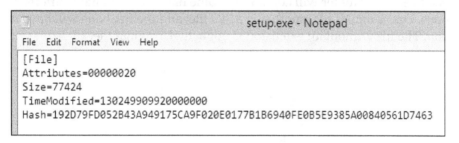

The folder structure is maintained within each package; however, every file will maintain the original filename but it will be an INI file with the information we have discovered. This will happen regardless of the file types, even if your package contains INI files themselves.

File library

The final part of the content library is the file library or FileLib. As the content library can span multiple drives on a distribution point, the files within the file library could be in any of these drives.

With only the first four characters of the hash, we get the file information in the data library folder. Within the file library, you will see a lot of folders. Find the folder name that matches our first four characters. We already have 192D; inside this folder, you will see the following three files:

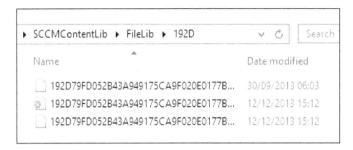

All of the files in this folder will contain the same name but will have different extensions. One is an INI file, another is a SIG file, and the final one will have no extension. The file without an extension is our actual, original file.

The INI file will contain a list of users; in this context, a user is a package that has the file. Where content has been subject to the single instance storage of the content library, then for a specific file you will see multiple users listed. The SIG file is not human readable and is used for the content validation function.

 Use the Content Library Explorer from the Configuration Manager Toolkit available from the Microsoft downloads website to have a tool to browse the library.

Content actions

Three actions are available on the content distributed to your distribution points. Each action has a different effect on the content and what happens during the distribution process. The first action is distribute. This is triggered on the initial distribution of the content to the distribution point. This action will distribute all of the files associated with the source path of the content; the exception to this is content that already exists. This will become subject to the single instancing process.

The next action is a content update. This is triggered when the **Update Distribution Point** option is selected in the console. This will transfer the changed files to all the distribution points. Unchanged files will not be transferred. If a file is removed from the package in the updated version, it will be deleted from the package on the distribution point, as long as no other packages are sharing it.

The final action is the redistribute action. This action is triggered when you select **Redistribute** in the console. Files will still be transferred and overwritten even if they are already present on the distribution point. The purpose of the redistribute action is to correct any inconsistencies that may exist in the content library.

Introducing network caching

Network caching is a technology that allows network devices or network appliances to cache content. If used effectively, this can allow organizations to use the caching device to deliver content to office locations where devices have poor network connectivity to where the master source of the content is located.

Common devices that use caching are Riverbed devices and Cisco WAAS devices, which stands for Wide Area Application Services. While you might think these devices could help with the deployment of Configuration Manager, they may actually cause you more pain than help.

It is really common to see these devices in large organizations; it is also common to think that you can use these to replace distribution points to deliver content to clients on slower sites.

Configuration Manager can, however, take advantage of BranchCache, which will enable a similar solution at a software level. This would be a recommended course of action if you are unable to deploy distribution sites to every location that requires them.

Recommendations for where caching devices exist

While network caching certainly has its uses in the enterprise, as far as Configuration Manager is concerned, it causes more problems. Content delivery to distribution points has been known not to work properly and cause problems. Likewise, the installation of site system roles to servers is where the traffic must traverse one of these devices.

 To prevent a troublesome deployment and potentially lots of time troubleshooting difficult and misleading error messages, exclude Configuration Manager traffic from the optimization or caching device.

Working with data deduplication

Windows Server 2012 introduced the ability to enable data deduplication on a volume to save storage and reduce the storage requirements for a file server. Thinking of Configuration Manager, two distinct uses are available for data deduplication. The first is the source location of our applications, packages, software updates, and operating system media. The second use is on the distribution point.

Deduplication on the content source

Essentially our content source is pretty much a file server, so you would think this is the perfect candidate for storage savings using deduplication. However, deduplication uses reparse points in the storage of data. Configuration Manager does not support the use of content sources that are stored on reparse points, so this is not a good candidate for enabling deduplication.

Deduplication on the distribution point

The content library within Configuration Manager does do small scale deduplication by using single instance storage; however, it does have some limitations. We can use deduplication to plug some of the gaps in single instance storage solutions.

The content library in Configuration Manager does the single instance storage using file-level single instancing, while deduplication uses chunk-level single instancing. You can potentially use deduplication where you use a large amount of operating system deployment content, such as **Windows Imaging Format** (**WIM**) files.

For the scenario where you distribute a new operating system image by updating some properties of an already existing image, only changed file blocks will be sent to the remote server when the **Enable Binary Delta Differential** option is enabled for the package. The entire changed file will be stored in the content library, even though the original and the revised file differ only by a few blocks. When deduplication is used in the same scenario, only a few extra blocks will be used to store the new data instead of the entire file. Configuration Manager will still send the complete package but the optimization will be on the storage of the distribution point server.

Evaluating data deduplication

Deduplication is very easy to set up on the server and is transparent to the applications using the data. As mentioned, the benefits of using deduplication are dependent on the type of files on a volume.

DDPEval is a tool available as part of the Windows Sever 2012 system (when the feature is turned on) that can be used to evaluate the space savings for a volume offered by the feature to decide if it's a candidate for enabling data deduplication. Additionally, this evaluation tool can be run on Windows 7 or later.

Summary

In this chapter, we have looked at how to manage content with Configuration Manager. We have gone all the way from setting up distribution points to understanding how the content library works and can help save us disk space by using single instance storage.

We also discovered how to create cloud distribution points in Windows Azure to save money by not having distribution points on server infrastructure. Finally, we looked at how to enable data deduplication on distribution points to further provide disk space savings on top of those provided by single-instance storage.

In the next chapter, we will look at the application model in Configuration Manager and how it can be used to deploy applications to your clients and how they differ from packages.

6
Application Deployment

So far we have discovered some of the big changes in Configuration Manager 2012. Arguably, none of them are as big as the chapter we are starting now. The introduction of the application model is a big change in the way we deploy applications. Applications contain lot more intelligence for the administrator to use when deploying their applications. We have the ability to manage the life cycle of the application to some extent.

In this chapter, we will be looking at the following topics as we look at how to deploy applications:

- Introducing the application model
- Deploying applications using the application model
- Deploying virtual applications
- How application management works
- When to use packages

Introducing the application model

As an administrator, you would be mistaken for thinking the application model is designed with you in mind and has been provided to make your job simpler. In a way, this is certainly the case; however, the application management model has an important place in Configuration Manager for users as well.

Applications in Configuration Manager support user-centric management and deployment so that you can associate specific users with specific devices. For example, you can deploy software to the user rather than the device and the deployment will be as effective as though you were deploying to a device. For many people, this was missing in the previous versions of Configuration Manager.

The deployment of applications with Configuration Manager is a state-based solution, which allows you to track the last deployment state for both users and devices. For example, much like the software updates we monitor for a specific state and then maintain that state, such as if it is uninstalled, we install it again.

Deployments are also evaluated on a regular basis by the Configuration Manager client; this allows us to support the following scenarios:

- If an application is uninstalled by the user accidentally or on purpose, at the next evaluation cycle, Configuration Manager detects this and reinstalls the application
- Requirements, such as disk space and operating system type, mean an application fails to install, however, a hardware change means the requirements are passed; Configuration Manager will now install the application
- We can also support both the installation and uninstallation of specific software using the application model

Application management workflow

The way we manage applications in Configuration Manager is a simple exercise. The process contains the following seven core functions that need to be performed:

1. Create the application.
2. Create one or more deployment types for the application.
3. Perform a simulated deployment (optional).
4. Deploy the application.
5. Monitor the application.
6. Deploy new versions of the application (optional).
7. Uninstall the application (optional).

Exploring the elements of an application

A typical application may contain some of the following aspects; not all of them are required but some are. These components help build up the capabilities of the application and make it a powerful deployment; some components are part of the deployment:

- Requirements
- Global conditions, which are used to build requirements
- Simulated deployment
- Deployment action
- Deployment purpose
- Revisions
- Detection methods
- Dependencies
- Supersedence

Using application requirements

Requirements on applications are nothing new. For long enough, we have known that our application requires 4 GB of memory and takes up about 300 MB of disk space. Using Configuration Manager, we can now specify these requirements.

One use of application requirements could be to replace complex collections. If a targeted resource does not match the requirements of the application, then it will not execute. This means that potentially you no longer need to create complex collections or queries to deploy your software; instead you can use collections that are broader. Most organizations still prefer to do this, think of your collection in this scenario as an extra safety net, which will give you that extra security that means you will still only target a subset of your resources.

Setting up a requirement is a simple process that is based on global conditions. You can use any of the built-in global conditions or create your own if you need to.

Requirements are set on the deployment type and not the application. Open your deployment type and click on the **Requirements** tab.

In this first example, let's create two requirements. The first is for disk space where we want more than 250 MB free on the system drive and the other is for at least 2 GB of memory. Click on **Add** to bring up the **Create Requirement** screen, as shown in the following screenshot:

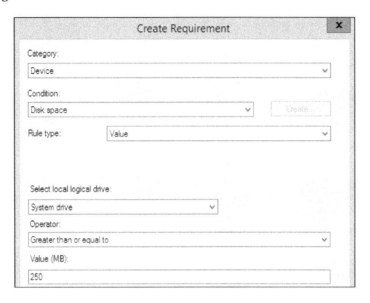

As you can see from the preceding screenshot, the process is really simple. Select the category as **Device** and the condition as **Disk space**, and then enter the required parameters. The process to add the requirement for memory is also very simple and quite similar.

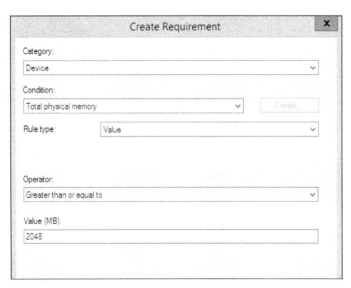

Simply select the condition as **Total physical memory** and again enter 2048 as the value, which is always in MB.

 Make sure you check the value that you input as it will always be in MB and not in GB. Check your input to avoid unexpected results.

You can then see your requirements listed in the console when you have finished. These requirements will then be evaluated when the device processes the deployment, as shown in the following screenshot:

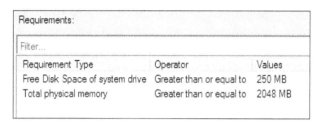

Requirement Type	Operator	Values
Free Disk Space of system drive	Greater than or equal to	250 MB
Total physical memory	Greater than or equal to	2048 MB

Using application dependencies

Lots of applications have dependencies, when you deploy these applications in the enterprise, it can be difficult to manage the deployment of dependencies. With Configuration Manager, you can deploy application dependencies at runtime.

When an application deployment is evaluated, part of this process includes the dependencies on the application. Configuration Manager will check whether the dependency is installed before deploying the parent application. The second action is that the application will not be installed if the dependency is not found.

This method can ensure that the application is installed and functions correctly without error due to missing prerequisites.

Dependencies for applications are also specified on the deployment type and not the application. Open the deployment type and click on the **Dependencies** tab.

 When you specify dependencies, they are specified in groups. The groups work by saying that if at least one of the requirements in a group is installed, then the dependency group is considered satisfied. If you have one dependency, then this is fine. However, if you have two dependencies and both of them need to be installed before the application, make sure you create them as separate groups, just like in the example we will run through.

Sample application deployment

Our application requires both the 32-bit and the 64-bit Visual C++ Redistributable packages to be installed. For this, we will create two dependency groups.

Enter the dependency group name. There are no hard rules for what you enter here, as long as people understand what it is. As you can see from the preceding screenshot, I added the 32-bit Redistributable application and said I want it to automatically install it, by checking the box.

In the preceding screenshot, you can also see that I have created another dependency group for the 64-bit edition of the Redistributable application. When you have finished entering these, the groups will be listed and will be connected with the AND operator.

With our dependencies set up, as shown in the preceding screenshot, the application deployment will ensure both are installed or else install them as required, before the application is installed.

Using application detection methods

A number of methods are available in Configuration Manager to specify how an installed application should be detected. If you are deploying a **Windows Installer package (MSI)**, for example, you can use the product code of the installer as the detection method.

You can also use the presence of a file or folder, for example, as well as a setting in the registry. You might also check for the specific value of a file or folder's properties.

The detection method helps Configuration Manager to determine whether the application needs installing on the target resource. Configuration Manager will evaluate the detection methods on an application before any content is executed and after the installation.

This is a big improvement on previous versions where we achieved the same thing using a custom bootstrap, such as a script before the installation, which was a lot of extra effort.

You can mix and match detection methods, for example, it is common to find executable installers that are actually bootstraps for an MSI installation. In this scenario, you can find the product code for the installer and use this code rather than finding out where in the registry or filesystem the application gets installed.

If you need to find out where an application has written to in the filesystem or registry, use Process Monitor from Sysinternals to find out this information (http://live.sysinternals.com/Procmon.exe).

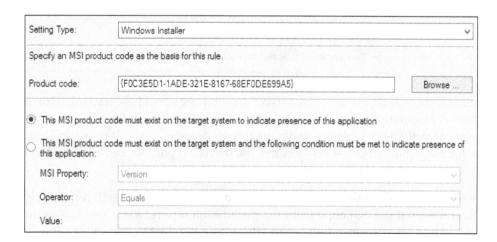

The preceding detection method is an example of an MSI product code for a Windows Installer. You get to this screen by clicking on the **Add Clause** on the **Detection Methods** tab of the deployment type.

From the setting type drop-down box, select **Windows Installer**. From here, you can enter the product code if you know it or point to an MSI file using the **Browse** button. When you use the file or folder method from the filesystem option, you can browse to a remote computer to select the file, as shown in the following screenshot:

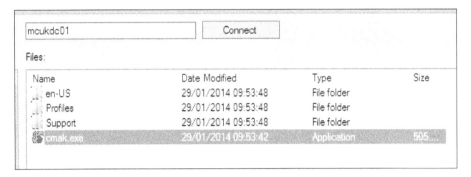

When you select the file, Configuration Manager will replace any common folder names with variables such as program files, application data, or other common locations. This will appear in the detection method screen, as you can see in the following screenshot:

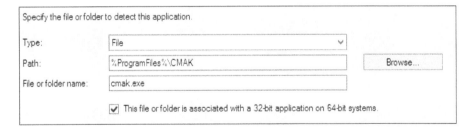

You must ensure that you have the correct state for the checkbox marked: **This file or folder is associated with a 32-bit application on 64-bit systems**. If you set this option incorrectly, then you may have the wrong detection rule. It may work on 32-bit, for example, but on 64-bit systems, the direction will not be redirected to the x86 Program Files directory.

This will cause the detection method to fail and your application will report a failed installation even if the exit code from the installation reports a success. We could potentially end up with an infinite loop attempting to reinstall the application. The same process as described earlier can be used when for registry settings as well.

If you have a complex set of detection rules, you need to check or want to look in WMI, for example. You can use a script detection, which will let you specify a PowerShell, VBScript, or JScript.

Using simulated deployments

A simulation of a deployment is exactly that it gives you the ability as an administrator to target your devices just as you normally would; however, the simulation will not install the application. This helps as we are not defining any logic in our collection membership, so the simulation is the only way to verify our logic is correct.

The device that receives the simulation will evaluate the detection method on the deployment type as well as the requirements and dependencies for a specific deployment type. The results of this process will be returned to the site where you can view them in the **Deployments** node in the **Monitoring** workspace.

Creating a simulated deployment is simple. From the ribbon or by right-clicking on the application, select **Simulate Deployment**.

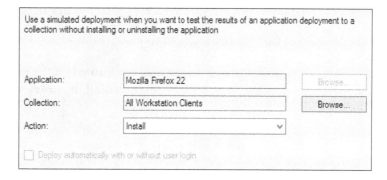

On the first screen that appears in the wizard, select the collection that you wish to deploy your simulation to and then specify the deployment action; this can either be install or uninstall.

Continue through the wizard and create the deployment. You can then monitor the simulation from the **Deployments** node in the **Monitoring** workspace.

Superseding applications

Configuration Manager allows you to upgrade or replace existing applications using a Supersedence relationship. When you supersede an application, you can specify a new deployment type to replace the deployment type of the superseded application and also configure whether to upgrade or uninstall the superseded application before the superseding application is installed.

How to specify a relationship

Open the application properties of the application that you are using to replace your old application. On the **Supersedence** tab, click on **Add** and then browse for the application that you wish to replace.

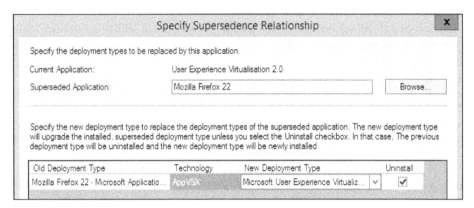

The preceding screenshot shows that, in this example, we are replacing **Mozilla Firefox 22** with the application **User Experience Virtualization 2.0**. Not a real-world example, but this shows how the configuration might look.

Make sure you select the new deployment type that will run when the replacement takes place, and for a clean deployment, ensure you uninstall the previous version you are replacing.

 Supersedence will affect available deployments as well. If you find a mistake and someone requires the old application, you will need to revert the configuration.

Targeting multiple platforms

Deployment types are used by Configuration Manager to specify the installation method of the application. You can use deployment types to create installation routines for multiple platforms. For example, you might specify an application that has deployment types for installation on Windows as well as iOS and Windows Phone. You may also have a deployment type for a web-based version of the application.

		User Experience Virtualisation 2.0		
Icon	Priority	Name	Dependencies	Technology Title
	1	Microsoft User Experience Virtualization Agent - X64	No	Windows Installer (*.msi file)
	2	Microsoft User Experience Virtualization Agent - X86	No	Windows Installer (*.msi file)

The preceding screenshot shows another example of this where we have created two MSI deployment types, both are obviously for a Windows operating system but we have a 32-bit and a 64-bit deployment. We are then using requirements to ensure the correct one is executed on the right system. In the previous versions, we would have created two collections and two advertisements to do this.

Making applications persistent

Sometimes you might want to make one of your applications persistent. A good example of this might be some security or monitoring software or another agent that you have deployed. Application management in Configuration Manager allows you to specify applications as required deployments. This means, if a user removes the application from the device, Configuration Manager will reinstall the application the next time a deployment evaluation is scheduled.

Right-click on the application and select **Deploy**. Select the setting you wish to on the **Deployment Settings** screen.

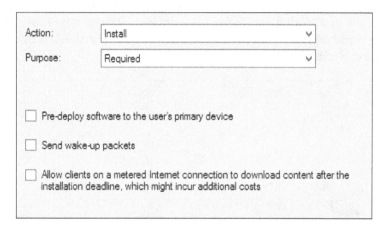

To ensure that the application will automatically be reinstalled upon evaluation should it be uninstalled, ensure that the **Purpose** drop-down box is set to **Required**, as shown in the preceding screenshot.

Deploying virtual applications

We can also use Configuration Manager to deploy virtual applications that have been sequenced using **Microsoft Application Virtualization (App-V)**. The benefits of using Configuration Manager to deploy your App-V sequences are that you do not have to deploy additional server infrastructure to manage the virtual applications.

All that is required is that the App-V client, which is part of the software assurance licensing, be deployed to the machines where you want to run App-V sequences and that the Configuration Manager client is also installed on the same machines.

The process is simple. We create an application that is an App-V type and select the appropriate version of the application, which we used to sequence our application.

Enter the UNC path to the App-V sequence file (. appv extension). This will be used to create the application and extract the properties from the sequence. You can go through and edit any properties you wish to add additionally or change them from the defaults.

When the application has been created, you can deploy it either for real or using a simulation like any other application.

App-V sequences are a great example of when to use dependencies. As we have already discussed, we need the App-V client to be deployed for the sequences to work. In your App-V applications, you can specify that a dependency is the App-V client. This will ensure that the client is always installed when a user tries to execute an App-V application, making the process seamless to the end user.

Using virtual environments

The virtual environments feature of Configuration Manager allows us to take full advantage of a feature in App-V known as connection groups. While the functionality is similar they do work in different ways.

Virtual environments are like sets in the Configuration Manager client; they are evaluated when the client performs an application evaluation cycle. When the client evaluates this to be true for two applications, the connection group is then created and deployed.

The curve ball here is that Configuration Manager virtual environments can only be a member of a single virtual environment at any given time. The virtual environment allows the App-V applications that we have specified in the virtual environment to share the same virtual filesystem and virtual registry.

How the application model works

Application management in the background is more complex than the way packages execute in Configuration Manager. The process works using **Configuration Items (CIs)**.

The following is a high-level overview of how the process works in order:

1. The client downloads the latest policy from the management point.
2. The client compiles the policy into WMI on the workstation.
3. The CCM Scheduler component notifies the DCM Agent about the activation of a task.
4. The DCM State Machine creates a new job in the CI Agent.
5. CI Downloader and the CI Store are then invoked to download the CIs associated with the application.
6. From the CI State Store, the metadata is downloaded to the CI State Store and the CI Models Store.
7. The **Policy Platform Client (PPC)** checks the requirements for the deployment type and dependencies.
8. PPC then invokes the application provider to invoke the correct handler, such as Windows Installer or the App-V handler.
9. Results on the process are handed off to the CI State Store.
10. A report is generated and the appropriate deployment type is selected based on the results.

The following diagram shows the relationship between the components involved in the delivery of applications using Configuration Manager:

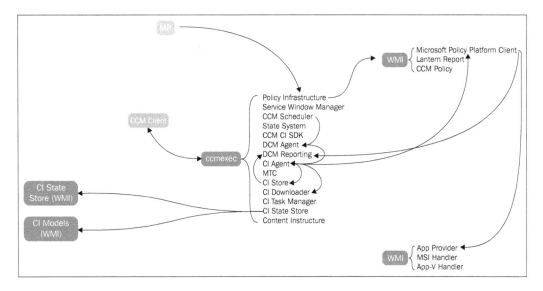

The diagram also lists all of the components within the Configuration Manager client and the components of WMI that are involved in this process; the components are as follows:

- Management point
- Configuration Manager client
- Configuration item state store
- Configuration item models
- Windows Management Instrumentation

When to use packages

With all this information of application management, you might wonder what the point in using packages is. Many customers of Configuration Manager still use packages as their primary deployment method.

I have heard a lot of reasons why people still use packages after their migration to Configuration Manager. One thing that is common after discussing this with customers is that reasons for sticking with packages are generally not valid.

The most common reason is that executable or batch files cannot be created as applications. This is simply not the case. Configuration Manager has a deployment type called script installer. The easiest way to think of the script installer is for anything else not listed in the drop-down box.

Uses for the script installer deployment type could be some of the following, which might be used to deploy applications:

- Executable
- InstallShield installers
- Batch files
- PowerShell
- VBScript
- JScript
- Custom bootstrap

Usage scenarios for packages

Packages do still have their place in Configuration Manager. After all, if they did not, then why is the feature still in the product? It could be for legacy support, which is a valid point; however, they do still have their place.

You may also use packages if you require running scripts from a distribution point support or scripts that you want to run on a schedule, applications will only execute once.

Operating system deployment is the biggest use of packages. We may need to copy files during the imaging process, which is a use for packages; another is other content or files we might need during imaging, that is, copying over registry files for example or a bunch of executables that we need to run in the process.

> Specific requirements may mean you need to use packages over applications; however, always think application first. Application management gives you the greatest set of capabilities and is highly flexible.

Summary

In this chapter, we explored the software distribution methods available to us in Configuration Manager. We looked at the way the application management works in Configuration Manager and why we would want to work with packages in certain scenarios.

In the next chapter, we will take a journey through the operating system deployment functionality of Configuration Manager, look at some real-world scenarios, and introduce some complexity into our task sequences.

7
Deploying Windows 8.1 and Windows Server 2012 R2

If you asked people to name a feature in Configuration Manager, the first one that would spring to mind for most people other than software distribution is probably operating system deployment. This functionality is a large part of Configuration Manager and is probably the most popular and the most supported by the community in terms of extensions and assistance available.

Configuration Manager can be used to deploy both desktop and server operating systems. In this chapter, we will run through the process of creating a reference image for both Windows 8.1 and Windows Server 2012 R2 that we can use to build desktops and servers. We will cover the following topics:

- Introduction to operating system deployment
- Integrating the Microsoft Deployment Toolkit
- Creating custom boot images
- Maintaining a driver library and packages
- Creating reference images
- Creating VHD files with task sequences

Introduction to operating system deployment

The ability to automatically deploy operating systems to a standard configuration in the enterprise is as important as the security on the endpoint. A standard environment means a secure and a stable environment.

Configuration Manager provides the ability to deploy standard operating system images created by the administrator in a repeatable manner to ensure that the deployment is the same time and time again making the operating environment consistent.

The following components are typical for most operating system deployment tasks:

- Boot images
- Drivers
- Driver packages
- Operating system image
- Applications
- Packages

Benefits of deploying standard images

Many people ask why it is worth the effort that is initially involved in developing a **standard operating environment** (**SOE**). The answer can depend on your interests within the organization.

Speak to someone in your security team and they will tell you that a standard environment is a secure one, which is predictable from a patching perspective. Speak to a service manager or someone in a support role and they will say that a standard environment will reduce the number of service desk calls as the environment is predictable from a management perspective.

A theme that is common in all the people you ask is that the environment is a predictable one. This comes from two angles, the first is that the environment is fully designed and developed like the implementation of a new system, so it is fully documented and the fundamentals are understood to the deepest level.

This understanding gives you absolute control and confidence that when you make any modifications, you know exactly what is affected and how it affects the running of the operating system.

Predictability is also good from a security perspective; an environment that runs standard software has a few exceptions in terms of permissions and access that is secure. This is true from a software level as well and is a reason why a corporate catalog of software is a really important piece of your whole management story.

Integrating the Microsoft Deployment Toolkit

For a long time Microsoft has had the ability to deploy operating systems outside of Configuration Manager. This has come in the form of a tool called the **Microsoft Deployment Toolkit (MDT)**.

MDT is a huge hit with organizations over numerous sectors and sizes. A big reason for this is that it is free; the other reason is that it is a massively flexible product that adds automation to your deployments.

Configuration Manager can also perform operating system deployment on its own as can MDT. The question is, "Which one do we use?" The answer is both. You can integrate the power of Configuration Manager and MDT with some console extensions for Configuration Manager allowing you to access task sequence templates and task sequence steps from the MDT product.

 MDT gives you a huge amount of extra capabilities and flexibilities so always download it and integrate it into your Configuration Manager environment; after all, it's free.

Starting with the R2 release of Configuration Manager, Microsoft has included some functionality that you will find in an MDT task sequence as a native functionality in Configuration Manager. A large gap in the abilities of both task sequence engines exists though, so it is still always worth installing MDT.

As with Configuration Manager, MDT is also updated frequently to provide support to the latest operating systems on both the desktop and server environments. The all-important download for MDT can be found on the Microsoft website at `http://technet.microsoft.com/en-gb/windows/dn475741.aspx`.

The first step is to simply download the MSI to your server and begin the installation wizard, as shown in the following screenshot:

All you need to do in the wizard is select the installation path; this would usually be the same drive that you have installed Configuration Manager to. Accept all the defaults in the wizard and the installation will complete. This should take no longer than five minutes.

> Integration of the MDT is purely optional; however, it does extend the capabilities that are already provided within Configuration Manager and allows you to do more complex tasks such as loading language packs and providing role-based configuration.

Installing the console extensions

When you have installed MDT, you need to install the console extensions, so the great functionality of MDT is available within Configuration Manager.

The first step is to launch the utility that is responsible for installing the console extensions; run this as administrator as a good course of action.

You should be able to find this utility by typing in `Configure ConfigMgr Integration` in the start screen in Windows Server 2012 or Windows Server 2012 R2 and by looking in the start menu under MDT on other operating systems.

When the screen comes up, the information about the site server and the site code is likely to be already populated for you, just as shown in the following screenshot:

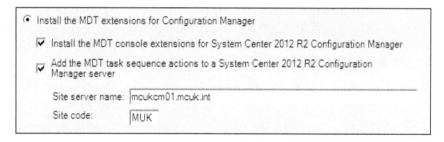

Validate whether the information on this screen is correct and click on **Next**. You should then be able to see a confirmation message displayed on the screen, which is similar to the following one:

Copied binaries for ConfigMgr 2012 to C:\Program Files (x86)\Microsoft Configuration Manager\AdminCor
Copied extension files for ConfigMgr 2012 to C:\Program Files (x86)\Microsoft Configuration Manager\Adr
Successfully connected to WMI namespace \\mcukcm01.mcuk.int\root\sms
Located the provider for site MUK on server mcukcm01.mcuk.int
Validated site server and site code.
Compiled C:\Program Files (x86)\Microsoft Configuration Manager\AdminConsole\\Bin\Microsoft.BDD.CI

Operation completed successfully.

When you have completed the integration wizard, close the **Deployment Workbench**. You can confirm that the console extensions have been added successfully by opening the Configuration Manager console, browsing to the **Operating Systems** node in the **Software Library** workspace and clicking on **Task Sequences**. Here, you should see a button on the left-hand side of the ribbon, which says **Create MDT Task Sequence**.

You can also navigate to the boot images node in the same area of the console where you should also see the text **Create Boot Image using MDT** on the ribbon.

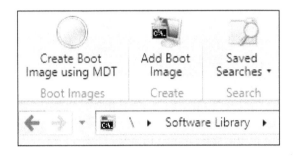

Configuring the deployment share

Another important and required stage of the installation and configuration of MDT is the creation of the deployment share. When you use MDT standalone, the deployment share is used to store the content used in the Deployment Workbench, which is the console used to control MDT.

In this example, we are going to create a simple deployment share so that we can access other functionality. Open the Deployment Workbench from the start menu.

When the Deployment Workbench is open, right-click on **Deployment Shares** and select **New Deployment Share**. Enter the path on your filesystem to where you want the deployment share created and then click on **Next**.

When you have entered the file path, you will be asked to supply a share name. This will be used to access the share over the network and acts just like a regular file share. Unless you have a specific reason to do otherwise, the default share name is just perfect.

Specify the share name to be used with the specified local path. If the share already exists on this computer, it must point to the path specified for this deployment share.

Share name:

DeploymentShare$

Full path UNC path: \\MCUKCM01\DeploymentShare$

When you have entered you share name, click on **Next**. Enter a descriptive name for the share if you wish or just accept the default. Continue through the wizard until the share has been created, at which point you should be presented with the following screenshot:

 The process completed successfully.

Creating share 'DeploymentShare$' with path 'E:\DeploymentShare'.
Share created successfully.
Performing the operation "New drive" on target "Name: DS001 Provider: Microsoft Deployment Toolkit\MI
Performing the operation "new" on target "deployment share".
Initializing a new deployment share
Initializing scripts and tools.
Performing the operation "open" on target "deployment share".
Deployment share at 'E:\DeploymentShare' opened successfully.
Adding MDT drive DS001 to the persisted drive list.
Successfully added MDT drive DS001 to the persisted drive list.

Configuring the deployment database

MDT also contains a database, which can be used to supply build information out of a database; this provides you, as an administrator, with a huge amount of power and flexibility for your deployments.

 The database can be useful to deploy language packs, set locale settings, such as the time zone and keyboard layout, as well as defining configuration for roles or specific models of devices. The use of the database is optional even when using the MDT.

For example, you can maintain a database entry for each machine to assist with the rebuild scenario of your machines or even better, maintain this information for a refresh scenario where you could replace the user's machine built specifically for them. The database offers many more uses; the limits are endless.

To create the database, you must have already created a deployment share. Open **Advanced Configuration**, right-click on **Database**, and select **New Database**.

In order to create a new deployment database, please provide the SQL Server details needed.

SQL Server name: mcuksql01

Instance: (optional)

Port: (optional)

Network Library: Named Pipes ⌄

Enter the database information that you need to connect to the database. If possible, use named pipes as the network library wherever possible. Named pipes will allow us to connect to the database from within the **Windows Preinstallation Environment (WinPE)** without the need to specify any credentials, which would need to be specified in plain text.

The reason for this is that WinPE is not aware of domain authentication; however, we can connect to a share using credentials, which allow us to connect to the database.

In order to make a SQL Server connection using Windows integrated security from Windows PE, it may be necessary to first establish a secure connection to the server. This is done by mapping a drive to the server. Specify the name of an existing share on the server that can be used to make this mapped drive connection.

SQL Share: DeploymentShare$ (optional)

Example: DeploymentShare$

In the preceding screenshot, you can see that we have entered the share name that we will connect to. This is done on the SQL Server; if you are running a remote SQL environment, then you will need to make sure this share is set up on your SQL environment.

Once the configuration has been completed, you will see a success screen similar to the one shown in the following screenshot:

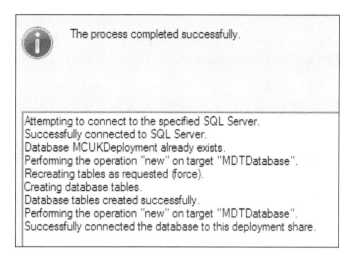

When this is completed, the database has been set up; you can look at the database setup from the deployment workbench, or via SQL Server Management Studio. It is managed out of the box using the deployment workbench; however, many community tools are available for managing the deployment workbench.

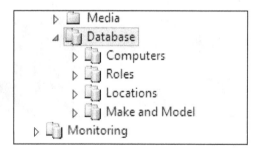

Creating custom boot images

When you deploy a Configuration Manager site, you will find that two boot images already exist in the console. These are created using the Windows Assessment and Deployment Toolkit or Windows ADK just like any other boot image.

Configuration Manager does not support the ability to create a boot image out of the box, unless you integrate MDT, in which case, you can then create your boot image from the console. Configuration Manager does, however, support adding custom boot images that have already been created. Without this interaction, we need the ability to build a boot image. This can be done using the .NET Framework along with the Windows ADK and some other utilities.

Before we begin with any scripting, the following few steps need to be completed:

1. Create a folder called `PEImage_x64`.

2. Then copy `winpe.wim` from the installation path of your ADK installation (`Windows Preinstallation Environment\amd64\en-us`) to the folder created in step 1.

3. Create another folder called `MountPoint` in the same drive as the first folder.

Now that this has been completed, open the **Deployment Tools and Imaging Environment** command line and mount the image using the following command:

```
Dism.exe /Mount-Image /ImageFile:E:\PEImage_x64\winpe.wim /index:1 /
MountDir:E:\MountPoint
```

When this command completes, you should see the following screen:

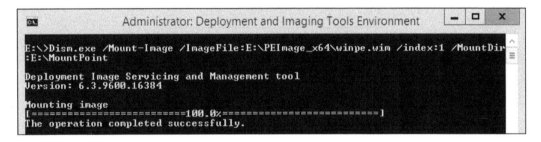

Next, use the same command prompt window to navigate to the directory that holds the components for the WinPE image (`C:\Program Files (x86)\Windows Kits\8.0\Assessment and Deployment Kit\Windows Preinstallation Environment\amd64\WinPE_OCs`).

From here, you can now add in components, such as MDAC, Scripting, .NET Framework, and PowerShell support.

You can do this by calling the following set of commands; each of them add the component to the mounted image:

```
dism /image:E:\MountPoint /add-package /packagepath:"WinPE-Scripting.cab"
```

```
dism /image:E:\MountPoint /add-package /packagepath:"en-us\WinPE-Scripting_en-us.cab"
```

```
dism /image:E:\MountPoint /add-package /packagepath:"WinPE-MDAC.cab"
```

```
dism /image:E:\MountPoint /add-package /packagepath:"en-us\WinPE-MDAC_en-us.cab"
```

```
dism /image:E:\MountPoint /add-package /packagepath:"WinPE-NetFx4.cab"
```

```
dism /image:E:\MountPoint /add-package /packagepath:"en-us\WinPE-NetFx4_en-us.cab"
```

```
dism /image:E:\MountPoint /add-package /packagepath:"WinPE-PowerShell3.cab"
```

```
dism /image:E:\MountPoint /add-package /packagepath:"en-us\WinPE-PowerShell3_en-us.cab"
```

When you have added all the components that you want to your boot image, you will need to execute the following command to unmount the image and commit the changes:

```
Imagex.exe /unmount /commit E:\MountPoint
```

When this is completed, you can then add your image into Configuration Manager.

Adding drivers to boot images

You will likely need to add network card drivers to your boot images at some point. This can be achieved in a few ways. The easiest is to look for the drivers that you require in your driver library and then simply right-click on it to select multiple drivers as well.

 When you add drivers to your boot image, you must make sure that they are for the correct version of WinPE and also the correct architecture.

In the context menu, you will see the option **Boot Images** under the **Edit** menu:

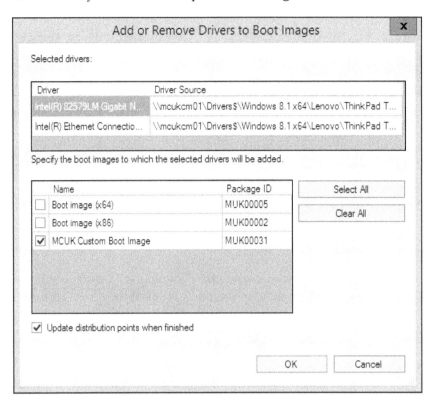

Check the boot image that you wish to add the drivers to and select **OK**. You can verify that the drivers have been added to your boot image by checking the properties of the boot image and looking at the **Drivers** tab. You should see your drivers listed in the window as shown in the following screenshot:

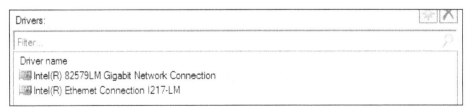

Adding components to boot images

Adding additional components to a boot image is also a simple task; this can be done by looking at the properties of a boot image by selecting the **Optional Components** tab.

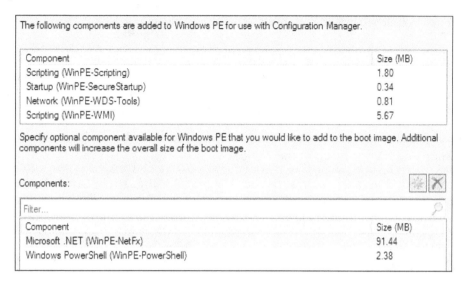

As you can see from the preceding screenshot, the components we specified when creating the boot image are here. Simply click on the starburst icon and select the additional components you require to add.

Maintaining a driver library

During a task sequence, Configuration Manager will apply drivers using one of two methods. The first is by using the task sequence step Auto Deploy Drivers and the second is by using the step Apply Driver Package. Essentially, both of these steps do the same thing; however, when you look at them in detail they work differently.

Auto Apply Drivers works by doing a plug-and-play enumeration of the devices, which are active at the time the operation takes place. This can be very effective as only the drivers that are required for devices that are currently active are installed. This can reduce the amount of bloat in your final deployment.

Using Auto Apply Drivers can however cause you to miss drivers and prompt the user to install them, which requires local administration rights meaning a call to the service desk. Using a driver package eliminates this problem.

> Auto Apply Drivers will also not work with standalone media as this relies on a query to the management point.

The reason for this is that when apply driver package is used, all the drivers are downloaded and stored in the local Windows driver store when the task sequence step is executed. This means when a device, which was not present at build time, is plugged in and we are shipping the driver only for that device, then it will be installed.

The prompt that appears asking for local administration rights is actually the driver installation and not the setup of the device.

Two realistic options are available to you. The first is using Apply Driver Packages and the second is to make use of the categories feature of the driver library. The first option has always been the most reliable one and produces results every time.

Managing drivers using driver packages

In order to make the management of your drivers a success, it is important to understand the following steps that are involved:

- Searching for and downloading the raw driver files from the vendor
- Extracting these drivers and creating the repository to store them
- Importing drivers into Configuration Manager, categorizing them, and creating driver packages
- Finally, assigning these driver packages to your task sequence

Searching and downloading drivers

Unfortunately, drivers are different depending on your vendor. Each vendor has their own tool for downloading drivers in the enterprise, the larger vendors such as HP, Lenovo, and Dell have their own tools, and some vendors have nothing, in which case, you will need to manually download the required drivers for your specific hardware models.

If you are an HP customer, then you can take advantage of their SoftPaq Download Manage utility, which is a free tool available from the HP website (`http://bit.ly/1kXQHOk`).

Lenovo also has a similar tool called the Update Retriever, which is part of the ThinkVantage administration tools. This is also a free download from the Lenovo website (http://lnv.gy/1euAgpQ).

Dell is slightly different in that rather than a utility to download the drivers, it has been prepared into cabinet or CAB files, which you can download. Again, these are free like the HP and Lenovo equivalents; you can find them on the Dell TechCenter (http://dell.to/1kXRtuP).

You can also use a tool from Dell called **Dell Client Integration Pack (DCIP)**. This allows you to integrate with the console so you can right-click and import drivers directly from the Dell repository. This tool can be very useful if you are using Dell hardware in your environment (http://www.dell.com/systemcenter).

Extracting drivers and creating a repository

One thing that is common between pretty much every hardware vendor is that drivers are delivered to match an operating system and a model. This means that your driver repository has a natural folder structure. First create a folder for your operating system, in our example, Windows 8.1 x64. Under this folder, create a folder for your vendor; some organizations run with multiple vendors which makes this structure easy to understand and simple to expand if required.

From here, create a folder for the model—it's that simple. You should have a folder structure similar to the one shown in the following screenshot:

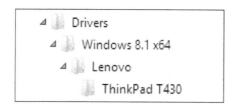

Some of your drivers might come in the format of a self-extracting executable or compressed file. If this is the case, extract them into the structure you have defined.

 Make sure you clean up your driver source. Some vendors ship multiple versions of the driver in one package. Just because the download is labeled **Windows 8.1 x64**, does not mean this is the only driver in the download.

Importing drivers into Configuration Manager

Now that we have downloaded and stored our drivers in a logical folder structure, it is time to import them into Configuration Manager. This process is simple and can be repeated easily for other models that you support in your environment.

Using the console in the **Software Library** workspace, right-click on **Drivers** from the **Operating Systems** node and then select **Import Drivers**.

Enter the UNC path to the source files in your driver library that you have created. Also, make sure that you select the option **Import the driver and append a new category to the existing categories**, as shown in the following screenshot:

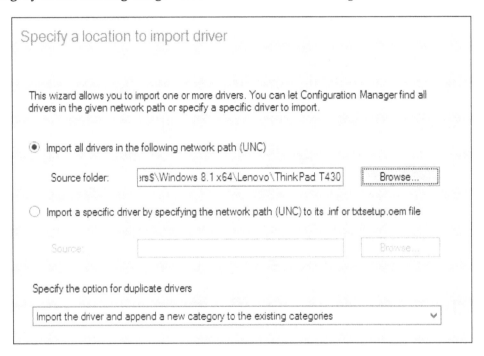

On the **Driver Details** page, click on **Categories** and create a category for the operating system and model of your device.

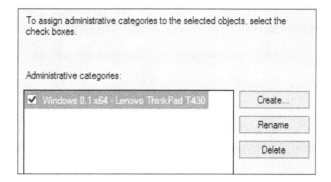

 If you are using your own internal version numbering for your deployments, then you could also use this here as well.

On the **Add Drivers to Package** screen, create a new driver package; provide the UNC path to where your source files will be stored for your driver package. It seems rather counterproductive to store the same drivers twice on the same server; however, you cannot create driver packages without importing drivers into the library first so this is unavoidable.

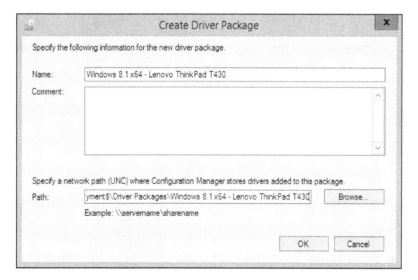

Once this information has been entered, then the wizard will import the drivers in the path that you have specified and also create the driver package. Don't forget you must also ensure that your content is distributed to your distribution point.

Assigning driver packages to task sequences

Depending on your vendor, it depends how you will format the WMI query that will be used to select the package. To make sure you have the right value, use the following PowerShell command line to make sure you have the correct string:

```
Get-WmiObject Win32_ComputerSystem | Select-Object Model
```

The output you can see in the next screenshot is the string you will need to enter in your task sequence.

In order to test the query you will use in your task sequence, you can also execute the following PowerShell snippet to allow you to test the exact query that you will use in Configuration Manager:

```
Get-WmiObject -Class Win32_ComputerSystem -Query "SELECT Model FROM
Win32_ComputerSystem WHERE Model LIKE '%P15xEmx%'"
```

Start off by opening the edit view of your task sequence. From here, navigate down to the **Apply Device Drivers** step, and either disable it or delete it. Add in a new step from the **Drivers** category and select **Apply Driver Package**.

Select the package that you have created for your device model, then in the **Options** tab, enter a new WMI query as shown here:

```
SELECT Model FROM Win32_ComputerSystem WHERE Model LIKE '%P15xEMx%'
```

You can also see from the following screenshot how this looks in the console as well:

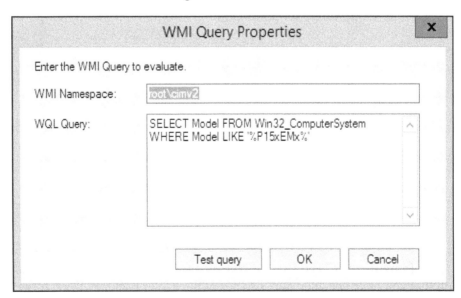

Ensure that you use the `like` statement in the query. This means your query will still work if the vendor changes the hardware model with a revision or any other data while you are still supporting it.

Creating reference images

Before you can deploy your operating system, you need to capture it. This is an important step; what you capture in your reference image will be the base to all of your corporate machines. It's important to make sure you think about what you want or need in this image.

For example, what Windows features do you want enabled or turned off in your image? Do you require any additional files such as a corporate background on the image? Do you need any additional information added into the registry?

 Your reference image is vitally important. Ensure that you discuss the details of the reference image with your peers and document what you have on your reference image and why it exists.

Another big decision is where you capture your reference image. Lots of people say capture your image outside of Configuration Manager using MDT, for example, or using the command-line tools available with the Windows ADK.

One reason for this may be the fact that when you deploy and capture your reference image using Configuration Manager, the client is baked into your image; this means it's difficult to use it anywhere else.

I like to keep my captured image development and the real-world deployment in one place wherever possible. If you need to use the image on another platform without the need for interaction with Configuration Manager such as a Citrix environment, for example, then this is a great example of when you would capture your image outside using MDT.

 Think carefully about the use of your image, as this will determine the way you capture your image.

Deciding on your image format

Another big decision that you need to make when thinking about your reference image is the type of output you are looking for; will you want or need a thin, thick, or hybrid image? Let's have a look at the differences.

Capturing and deploying thick images

A thick image is where all of your applications go into one image. This can have benefits depending on the sort of environment you are deploying your image to. If you are deploying to a fixed environment, which also has a static number of applications that do not update that often, then a thick image may be the way to go.

With a thick image, all of your applications are in the same image as are all of your standard Windows and application patches. This makes the deployment process very repeatable and very quick.

Thick images also have their downside. The biggest problem with a thick image is that every time an application update is required, you need to capture the image again. Quickly you can be in a situation where you are releasing new versions of your image every few months.

This approach is neither practical nor is it a good use of your time. Additionally, this may mean that configuration drift is difficult to control and manage with different versions of the same image in your environment.

Capturing and deploying thin images

A thin image in deployment terms is as you would expect from the name. This image contains only the bare minimum; this is usually just the modified version of Windows that your organization uses and the updates that you require.

The advantage with this image over a thick image is that it is easy to maintain, easy to update, and is less likely to cause you issues further down the line as you are only applying more updates to the image.

Another advantage is that any applications you add in your task sequence can be changed easily without having to capture the full image again and causing numerous issues further down the line.

A reason for not using a thin image could be the speed at which you need to do your deployment. If you have lots of applications, some of them large in size, this may make your deployment longer as the content will need downloading before it can be installed.

If time is a critical factor in your deployment, then you may want to look at alternatives to a thin image. While it might be the best technical solution, it might not fit your organization's requirements.

Capturing and deploying hybrid images

A hybrid image for many is the best of both worlds. It combines the advantages of a thin image, which is light on content, with the advantages of a thick image, which is mainly deployment time.

Your hybrid image may contain one or two applications, which are not updated frequently but are needed by everyone in your organization. Office is a great example of this as might be framework applications or clients such as your antivirus.

The advantage of using a hybrid image with Office, for example, is that it can be updated like Windows and can use the same tools to include the latest patches. Your image can easily be deployed and maintained where required and you also maintain the speed of deployment to some degree, since using the Office example you are not having to deploy one of your biggest applications.

 A hybrid image will fit many organization requirements and might be the one for you. Test the method you choose to make sure it works before you commit to it.

Maintaining versions on your images

You would usually associate source control with programming and application development. Actually, source control is everywhere in IT including document management. Your images should be no different.

It is important just like with source code to manage the versions of your image and keep a record of what has been changed. This will let you easily identify issues should any arise as people will instantly know what has changed.

A great way to manage versions in images is to tattoo the image when you capture it by writing some keys to the registry. This is a simple task that is effective and can be used in many other things in your management strategy, such as planning upgrades and finding out who has older versions of your corporate image still out there.

The easiest thing to add is the version number of the build. This can be anything you want but the simplest way is to use traditional version numbers where we would specify the major, minor, and release version, for example, something like 2.1.12. You should also add a timestamp of when the image was captured. This is just a good way to keep track of when the image was created along with the version number.

This can easily be done in your capture task sequence, for example, by using a PowerShell script. To achieve this simply, use the following script that will set the current date and time to English UK format and then create our new key as well as two string values, which contain the version number and the timestamp of when the deployment is captured:

```
$DateTime = Get-Date -Format "dd/MM/yyyy HH:mm:ss"
New-Item -Path HKLM:\SOFTWARE\MCUK -Name Tattoo -Force
New-ItemProperty -Path "HKLM:\Software\MCUK\Tattoo" -Name BuildVersion
-PropertyType String -Value "8.0.0"
New-ItemProperty -Path "HKLM:\Software\MCUK\Tattoo" -Name BuildTimeStamp
-PropertyType String -Value $DateTime
```

Save this as a regular PowerShell script, add it to a package, and you can then call it from within the task sequence as shown in the following screenshot:

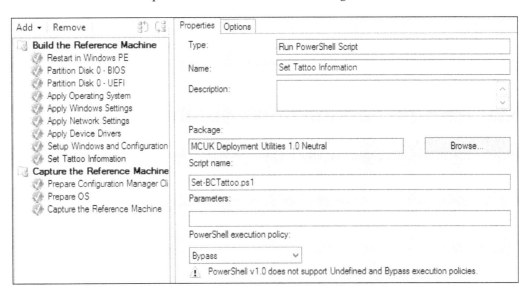

Using images in virtual environments

Starting with Configuration Manager 2012 R2, the ability has been added to create virtual images; once they have been created, these can then be uploaded to the library server in **Virtual Machine Manager** (**VMM**), which is also part of System Center used for managing virtualized server environments.

Before you begin, a number of prerequisites should be met, which are as follows:

- You must use one of the following operating systems to manage the images:
    - Windows 8.1 x64
    - Windows 8 x64
    - Windows Server 2008 R2
    - Windows Server 2012
    - Windows Server 2012 R2

- Virtualization must be enabled in the BIOS so Hyper-V can be installed; you should also install the Hyper-V management tools

Once the preceding prerequisites are in place, you are ready to start creating virtual images.

Creating VHD files using task sequences

The first question here is, "Why create your **virtual hard disk** (**VHD**) files in Configuration Manager and then upload them to VMM?" The answer is that as we move away from physical server builds, we still need to provision servers, which are running a common image to our physical servers. While VMM provides the ability to import images, it does not provide the ability to create images.

This method allows us to apply the same rules to server images in the virtual world as we do with desktops and laptops in the workstation world. This allows us to apply the same thought process to create images to be used in templates in VMM to allow us to not only deploy standard VM templates and VM services but also mean that the core Windows image underneath is also standard across your whole virtual server estate.

Creating the task sequence for the VHD

Creating the task sequence is a wizard driven operation just like a regular task sequence. Right-click on **Task Sequences** and select **Create Task Sequence**. From the options, select **Install an existing image package to a virtual hard disk**, as shown in the following screenshot:

A task sequence performs multiple steps or actions on a client computer at the command-line level without requiring user intervention. Select the type of task sequence to create. You can use the task sequence editor to add steps to your task sequence.

Select a new task sequence to be created.

○ Install an existing image package

○ Build and capture a reference operating system image

◉ Install an existing image package to a virtual hard disk

○ Create a new custom task sequence

The wizard is the same as creating a regular task sequence; you will be asked for an existing image, the client package, and whether you want to add any applications.

You will notice that at the end of this task sequence is a shutdown command. This is added so that Configuration Manager can capture the image into a VHD; this cannot be done while the machine is booted into Windows.

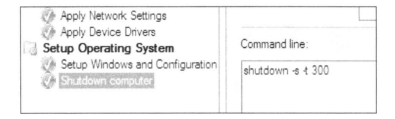

Creating the VHD

Hyper-V must be installed on the computer running the Configuration Manager console from which you manage VHDs or the **Create Virtual Hard Disk** option is not enabled in the Configuration Manager console.

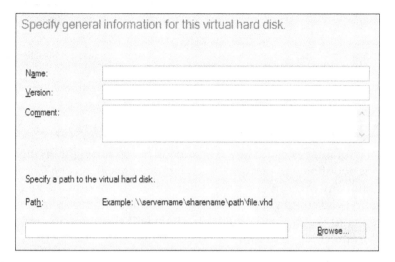

Insert a **Name**, **Version**, and **Comment** (only the name is required) and the **Path** to where the virtual hard disk will be created. Then, just like the prestaged media wizard, select the task sequence from the **Browse** button.

Run through the wizard providing distribution points and any customization that you might require; when the wizard completes, you will see the following progress bar:

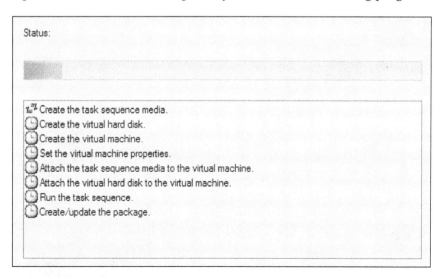

During this process, you can connect to the console in Hyper-V to see how the task sequence is progressing. Upon completion, the hard disk will be shown in the console; from here you can schedule updates like a regular image as well as upload the VHD to Virtual Machine Manager.

Deploying your captured images

The deployment of images could be a whole book in its own right. In this section, we will get an idea about how to perform basic deployments just using Configuration Manager without any MDT integration. While this does not provide you with the full functionality, you could get by having both Configuration Manager and MDT working together. It is still a powerful tool, which will allow you to deploy your operating environment in a simplified and unified manner.

The most basic of task sequences can be put together fairly quickly using Configuration Manager. This will give you the ability to deploy your image, install and update Windows that you might need, and add your client to the domain or a workgroup. You will even be able to deploy additional applications and migrate user state if you wish.

In the **Software Library** workspace, you will see **Task Sequences** under **Operating Systems**. On the ribbon, click on **Create Task Sequence**, where you will be presented with a wizard, as shown in the following screenshot:

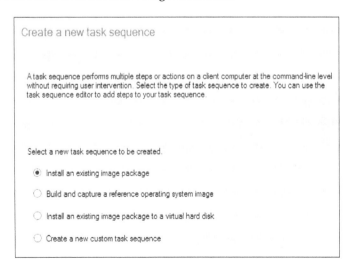

In the new wizard which appears, we have a number of options; in this example, we will select the top radio button that states **Install an existing image package**. This allows us to deploy an image that we have already captured or an image prepared by someone else.

Configuring the task sequence information

On the **Task Sequence Information** screen, we need to provide a name for the task sequence. This will be visible when the task sequence is running so it needs to be short and descriptive. We can however override what is shown here once the task sequence is created.

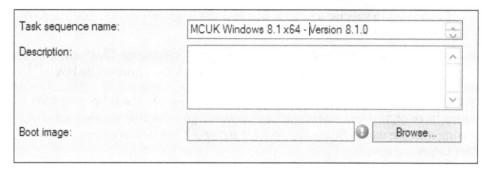

You can also provide a description for the task sequence. This information will not be displayed and is purely for administrators who have access to the console. Before continuing to the next step, we also need to select a boot image.

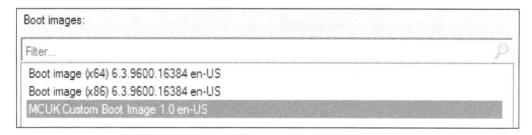

Your boot image will be used when the task sequence goes into WinPE and will contain network drivers to allow your boot image to connect to the network.

 Boot images with an x64 architecture can only deploy x64 operating systems; however, x86 boot images can deploy both x86 and x64 operating systems.

On the **Install Windows** page, we have to specify a number of options to allow us to install our Windows image:

1. Select the image package that you have loaded into Configuration Manager.

2. If the image package contains multiple images, ensure that you select the correct one from the **Image** drop-down box.

3. Check the box **Partition and format the target computer** if you want Configuration Manager to add in a task sequence step for preparing the drives on the target computer.

4. If you require the use of BitLocker, then make sure you check the box **Configure task sequence for use with BitLocker**.

5. If you need to specify a license key and the licensing mode, then do so on the following two boxes.

6. Finally, if you want Configuration Manager to disable the local administration account and then set a random password, check the appropriate box.

The preceding configuration that we have set can be seen in the following screenshot where we have picked our image package and image as well as configured the formatting and the use of BitLocker. We are using a KMS in this example, so no product key is required.

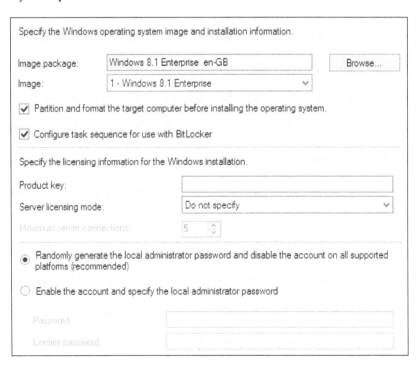

Next, we need to select where we want the machine placed on the network; do we want it in a workgroup or on the domain. If you want to join the client to a workgroup, then simply enter the name of the workgroup.

For domain-joined machines, you will need to select a domain and an **organizational unit (OU)** for the client to join. You must then specify an account that has permissions to join the client to that specific OU.

 Active Directory has a default container called computers. This cannot be used as it is a container and not an organizational unit; selecting the computers container will result in the task sequence failing.

We are then asked to provide information on the installation of the Configuration Manager client. Here, you can specify additional properties that you would usually set when installing the client.

If you have configured **user state migration (USMT)** using the configuration files within USMT, then on the **Configure state migration** screen you can specify additional options and set the configuration for the backup and restoration of a user's state.

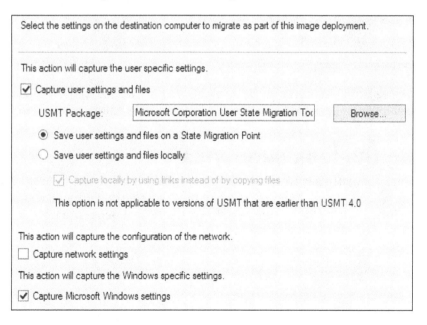

As you can see from the preceding screenshot, we have selected to use the state migration point to store our content rather than storing it locally. We have also selected options to allow us to capture settings from Windows. This includes the date and time information and locale information.

In the final two steps, we can select if we want Windows updates to be deployed; here we have three options:

- Mandatory software updates
- All software updates
- Do not install any software updates

For this step to work, updates must be downloaded and available. We do not have to create a deployment for the updates to be installed during the task sequence. Finally, we can then select applications that we want to be deployed as part of the task sequence.

As you can see from the preceding screenshot, we have added in the Visual C++ 2013 Redistributable package to be deployed in our task sequence.

Editing the task sequence

Once the task sequence has been created, you can edit it using the task sequence editor. This will allow you to revisit some of the configuration options you provided during the initial setup without the need to create the task sequence from scratch.

We can also add new steps or remove old ones using the task sequence editor. A number of task sequence steps are available for performing a number of actions, such as deploying drivers to running command lines and setting variables for use in our task sequence to installing software.

The task sequence that we have just created should look similar to the one in the preceding screenshot. We have replaced the default autoapply drivers step with a driver package and added a condition as we discussed earlier in this chapter.

Making your task sequence available

When you are happy with your task sequence, you will need to distribute the content to your distribution points. You can select the task sequence and click on **Distribute Content** on the ribbon or by right-clicking on the task sequence. This wizard will guide you through deploying all of the referenced content in your task sequence.

Finally, you must create a deployment that will allow your clients to execute the task sequence. Task sequences can only be deployed to device collections and not user collections.

 Try to avoid deploying to unknown computers unless you have a method of preventing the task sequence from executing mandatory, such as a password or just making the task sequence available.

When you have created the deployment for your task sequence, you are ready to begin deploying it to your clients.

Summary

In this chapter, we have taken a somewhat high-level look at the basics of capturing images to use in operating system deployment. We have also discussed what type of image you might want to use in this process as well as looking at integrating with the Microsoft Deployment Toolkit.

We have also looked at how to manage a driver library in Configuration Manager as well as looking at how to create virtual hard disks in Configuration Manager, which can be used in your virtualization environment and even uploaded to Virtual Machine Manager.

In the next chapter, we will be looking at how to use the software update functionality of Configuration Manager to apply security updates to your environment as well as deploying patches for products, which may have been written in house or by third-party products.

8
Deploying Security Updates

A critical part of systems management and an important part of any systems management strategy is the ability to manage and deploy security updates on managed devices. Configuration Manager has the ability to deploy and manage security updates on devices and also introduces functionality such as maintenance windows and some advanced settings to control the patching cycle on your devices.

In this chapter, we will look at the design of an update infrastructure as well as looking at sample scenarios to manage your updates on both servers and workstations. We will cover:

- Designing a software update infrastructure
- Monitoring software updates
- A sample scenario for workstation patching
- A sample scenario for server patching

Software updates

Before we start looking at and discussing the infrastructure that is required to deploy software updates in Configuration Manager, it is important to understand the terms used in software updates as well as discuss the capabilities of Configuration Manager in terms of software update deployment.

You can deploy software updates in an enterprise environment using **Windows Software Update Services (WSUS)**. This is a free tool from Microsoft, which is a server role within Windows Server. Once installed, you can manage and deploy updates to managed clients.

As you are already using Configuration Manager, you can also leverage this functionality from within Configuration Manager, which also takes advantage of the WSUS technology.

The difference between the two implementations is that as a standalone system, WSUS will manage and deploy updates; however, when used with Configuration Manager, WSUS is used to download the update manifest from Microsoft. Configuration Manager is then responsible for downloading the updates and deploying them. The distribution points in your hierarchy will be responsible for hosting the software update packages, which the clients will obtain via the Configuration Manager client, just like a regular software distribution package.

> Along with downloading the manifest, this also contains detection logic for clients so the client knows which updates to apply.

The anatomy of software update deployment

The deployment of software updates works using the same principles as application deployment, package distribution, and task sequence deployment, in that they are all targeted to collections.

Along with collections, you will also come across the following terms when we talk about software updates:

- Software update groups
- Deployment packages
- Automatic deployment rules
- Deployments

Introducing software update groups

Software update groups are used to contain selected updates, which you will deploy to your clients. You can filter the updates that you want to deploy from the **All Software Updates** node in the console using the search and filter capabilities.

When you have added updates to a group, you can then act on the group by downloading and/or deploying the updates to a specific collection. You can also use update groups as a reference to report compliance.

Introducing deployment packages

Deployment packages are the result of downloading the content associated with a software update group. When you choose to download a software update group, you can select to add the content to either an existing software update package or a new software update package.

When a deployment package has been created, this is then distributed to the selected distribution points so the content can be served to clients.

 You cannot distribute software update packages to cloud distribution points. However, you can configure clients to fall back to Windows update.

As the content is processed from the site, it will be subject to the single instance storage that is part of the distribution point. This may help you reduce your storage space requirements for content that is distributed to the distribution points in your hierarchy.

Introducing automatic deployment rules

You can use an automatic deployment rule to automatically approve and deploy software updates. Automation is a key method for the deployment of monthly software updates (**Patch Tuesday**) and to deploy definition updates for **System Center Endpoint Protection**.

When the automatic deployment rule is run, the software updates that meet the specified criteria are added to a software update group, the content files for the software updates are downloaded and copied to distribution points, and the software updates are deployed to client devices in the target collection.

How software update synchronization works

Software update synchronization in Configuration Manager uses a connection to Microsoft Update to retrieve information on software updates, known as metadata. The top-level site (central administration site or standalone primary site) will synchronize with Microsoft Update on a schedule defined in the component configuration (known as a full synchronization), or when you manually start the synchronization from the Configuration Manager console (known as delta synchronization).

When Configuration Manager has completed the software update synchronization on the site, the synchronization will begin on the child site(s), should one exist. When the synchronization is complete on each primary site or secondary site in the hierarchy, a site-wide policy is created that provides the location of the software update points to clients in the hierarchy.

The following steps are a basic outline of how synchronization works on the top-level site:

1. The synchronization manager will send a request to the instance of WSUS running on the software update point to start.

2. The metadata is synchronized from Microsoft Update, and any changes that are needed are inserted or updated in the database.

3. When the synchronization in WSUS has completed, the metadata from the database is synchronized with the Configuration Manager database. Metadata is stored in the database as configuration items.

4. If any child sites exist, then the synchronization manager sends a request to all the child sites.

Synchronization on child sites

After the process of synchronization is complete on the top-level site, the site will send a notification to all child sites to begin synchronization on them.

The process is similar to a parent site; however, the synchronization is run from the software update point on the parent site. Here is the full process that takes place on the site:

1. The synchronization manager receives a request from a top-level site.

2. The synchronization starts on the child site.

3. WSUS, on the software update point of the child site, synchronizes metadata from the parent site.

4. If the child site is a primary site and has a secondary site(s), then a request to synchronize will be sent to this site, only if the secondary site has a software update point.

Designing a software update infrastructure

The deployment of software updates is critical to maintaining efficiency and security as well as stability in an enterprise environment. Due to the nature of technology and its ever-changing landscape, the threats associated with this are also changing constantly. An effective software update process requires consistent and continual attention.

Making sure you design a software update infrastructure within Configuration Manager that is fit for purpose is also an important part of ensuring that you are able to deliver updates to clients in a manner that is efficient, protects your environment as quickly as possible, and more importantly, does not disrupt usual business activities.

One of the biggest complaints about IT departments is that when patches are deployed, the need to reboot is often forced upon the user.

Capacity planning of the software updates infrastructure

The number of clients that are supported depends on the version of WSUS that runs on the software update point. Another factor that determines the number of clients is dependent on whether the software update point co-exists with another site system role, such as a distribution point or management point:

- You can support up to 25,000 clients when you use WSUS 3.0 Service Pack 2 on the software update point and where it co-exists with another role

- You can support up to 100,000 clients when you use the same configuration as mentioned previously and the software update point role does not co-exist with another site system role

In the first configuration, you can use an NLB to support more than 25,000 clients. For the second configuration, to support more than 100,000 clients, you need to meet the hardware requirements defined for WSUS (`http://technet.microsoft.com/en-us/library/cc708483(WS.10).aspx`).

You can also deploy multiple software update points like you can with management points to help distribute the load.

 The number of updates that exist in a deployment must not be more than 1,000 objects. If you create an automatic deployment rule that specifies more than 1,000 objects, then the rule will fail.

How to design the infrastructure for software updates

Before you even begin to design the infrastructure for the environment you are managing, a number of available prerequisites that are both internal and external to Configuration Manager. You need to make sure these requirements are satisfied in order for software updates to operate properly.

The following requirements are internal to Configuration Manager:

- The management point
- The software update point
- The distribution point
- Client settings that are properly configured for software updates
- The reporting services point, which is optional but highly recommended

The following dependencies are also required, but these are external to Configuration Manager:

- IIS on the server designated to run the software update point
- The installation of WSUS
- The WSUS administration console on the site server (if you are installing a remote software update point)

Planning the placement of software update points

The central administration site and all child primary sites must have a software update point where you want to deploy updates. You will also need to consider whether you need to service clients on the Internet. If this is the case, you will need a software update point that accepts communication over the Internet. If your hierarchy contains secondary sites, you will have to consider the need for software update points at secondary sites as well.

Starting from Configuration Manager 2012 SP1, you can add multiple software update points at the primary site level. This configuration provides the ability to add fault tolerance without the need to set up NLB.

While you can use multiple software update points to provide some load balancing, the solution is not as stable or robust as using NLB. The failover design that is used for software update points is different from the one used in management points. Unlike the design of management points, when a client switches between software update points, client and network performance costs are associated with this action.

 Use multiple software update points from a fault tolerance perspective. If you require true load balancing, then stick to using NLB as it provides a much more stable and robust balancing solution.

Just like when you design a site hierarchy, designing the infrastructure that will support your software update needs is important and requires thought. Just like deciding where to place management points, distribution points, and secondary sites, the placement of software update points requires consideration.

Using an existing WSUS server as the source

If your corporate security policy does not allow access to the Internet from your primary site or central administration site, then you can use an existing WSUS server that is located in your DMZ environment as the source server for the top-level synchronization.

You can see an example of this configuration in the following diagram:

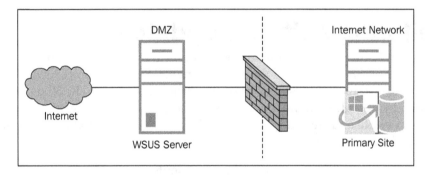

In the preceding diagram, you can see that the WSUS server in DMZ is acting as the source for the primary site in the internal network. Traffic is routed through a firewall. If you are setting up your environment in this way, then make sure you set up the correct firewall ports to be open.

Depending on your setup, you will require either ports 80 and 443 to be open or 8530 and 8531 to be open. They will need to be open from the software update point to the source server.

Planning for the switching of software update points

If you have multiple software update points at any specific site and one fails or becomes unavailable, clients will connect to a different software update point and continue to scan for the latest software updates. When a client is assigned a software update point, it will stay assigned to that software update point unless it fails to scan for updates.

When a scan on the client fails with a retry code, the client starts a process to scan for updates on a software update point. When a client fails a scan, the following process will be used:

1. The client scans for updates at a scheduled time or when a user initiates the action via the Control Panel or using PowerShell. If the scan fails, the client will retry in 30 minutes using the same software update point.

2. After four retries at 30-minute intervals, following the final retry plus 2 minutes, the client will move to another software update point, as determined by the software update list.

3. Following a successful scan, the client will continue to connect to the software update point.

Monitoring software updates

Configuration Manager contains a number of built-in reports that enable you to view information on the status of your deployments, the compliance level of your clients, the scan status, and also perform some troubleshooting. The 30 reports that are shipped by default with the reporting services point installation give you a great view of your estate and should give you all the information that you need to report on your patch compliance.

You can also perform the monitoring of deployments and the compliance of a specific path or update group using the Configuration Manager console, which also displays some basic data.

Viewing compliance using reporting

Configuration Manager contains a number of reports to monitor the compliance of your clients. The following categories are available for reporting:

- Software Updates – A Compliance
- Software Updates – B Deployment Management
- Software Updates – C Deployment States
- Software Updates – D Scan
- Software Updates – E Troubleshooting

Each of the five categories contain a number of reports that are aimed at providing you with the information you need to assess compliance, manage your deployments, view scan states for your environment, and perform troubleshooting.

The scan and troubleshooting reports are useful to find out when clients are not reporting the scan state to a software update point.

Monitoring compliance with baselines

You can use another function of Configuration Manager called compliance settings to also monitor the compliance of software updates in your environment. You can create a configuration baseline that contains your baseline software updates; this baseline can be deployed to a collection, and its progress and compliance can be monitored in the console or in further detail using the reporting functionality.

The **Compliance and Settings Management** category in the **Reporting** node contains 17 reports to look at the status of compliance baselines. The following reports are useful when looking at update compliance:

- The compliance history of a configuration baseline
- Summary compliance by configuration baseline
- The summary compliance of a configuration baseline for a collection

A sample scenario to patch workstations

In this section of the chapter, we will take a look at a scenario for patching workstations. Before we begin, we need to lay out some information about what our customer wants in terms of requirements, just like a full design; these details that we'll gather here will be important for us to make decisions for the design of the patching solution.

Customer requirements

In this scenario, our customer will deploy patches to workstations on a monthly cycle. This cycle will closely align with the Patch Tuesday concept, as follows:

- Deployments will be created and sent to a pilot group of workstations once a week after the patches are released by Microsoft.
- Following the deployment of patches to a pilot group, the deployment will then be sent to the remainder of the workstations.

- Portions of the process need to be automated to reduce administrative effort.

- Only critical updates and security updates are required for Windows 8.1 and Office 2013. No third-party or in-house updates are required.

- The solution needs to be implemented using existing equipment.

- The administrator should be able to report on patch compliance on either a monthly, quarterly, or yearly basis.

The organization has a simple Configuration Manager 2012 R2 hierarchy, with a single, standalone primary site that has 15,000 devices over two office locations. Both offices are well connected to the primary site, which is located in a managed data center by a third party.

Implementing the infrastructure for patching

As we have already discovered, our organization already has a simple hierarchy. To enable us to start deploying software updates, we first need a software update point. We have two options for the software update point architecture. The first is to simply deploy a single software update point on the primary site, and the second option is to create an additional software update point to provide fault tolerance.

Deploying a single software update point

Now, let's have a look at our first option, which is to deploy a single software update point in the environment. The software update point will be deployed on the server that is currently hosting the primary site.

With this configuration, we provide support for up to 25,000 clients as the primary site also hosts some additional site system roles. With this configuration, we will be able to have the software update point co-exist with existing roles. That is why we can support up to 25,000 clients and not 100,000.

The disadvantage of deploying a single software update point is that we have no fault tolerance should the server be unavailable. However, as we are planning to deploy the software update point on the primary site, with the primary site unavailable, we would not be able to manage the site.

The following diagram shows how the final architecture might look once the environment has been designed:

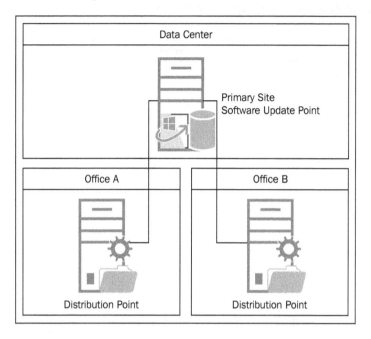

This solution allows all the requirements to be met, and most importantly, addresses the requirement to keep costs low.

Deploying multiple software update points

Now, we will discuss the second option of using multiple software update points. In this solution, we will deploy a software update point alongside the existing distribution point and management point server at each office location.

While this solution provides fault tolerance, and each office has good links to the data center, this solution does present us with a couple of issues.

The first issue is that we are at a real danger of over-engineering the solution based on the requirements. None of our requirements need fault tolerance or load balancing; while it is considered good practice to provide fault tolerance where possible, we also have a requirement to use existing equipment and keep costs low.

The second issue with this solution is that while we can place two software update points, one in each office, we have no guarantee that clients at **Office A** will communicate with the software update point at that office.

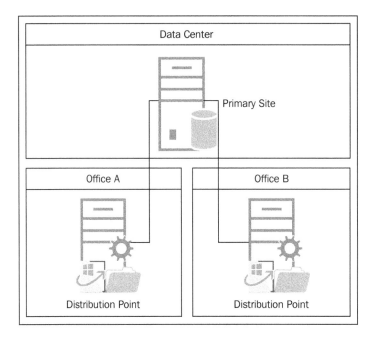

As you can see from the preceding diagram, this solution presents the same options as the previous solution. We tick all the requirements as we are placing the software update points on existing servers, so we are not purchasing any new equipment.

We also require WSUS Administration Console installed on the primary site to be able to use the functionality that is required.

Software update point design decisions

With the information we have been given and taking into account both of the options available to us, we have made a decision to go with the first option, which is to deploy a single software update point on the primary site.

We have picked this solution for the following reasons:

- It meets all the stated requirements
- It is simple to set up and administer
- It keeps additional roles and setup to a minimum

The same points could probably be said for the second design option too; however, this option does provide extra complexity and give us way more than the number of supported clients that we require.

Configuring the software update point component

For this example, we will assume that the software update point is installed and configured. Before we can configure the deployment aspect of the solution, we need to configure the software update point component on the site, as follows:

1. We open the configuration by going into the **Sites** node within **Site Configuration** in the **Administration** workspace.

2. From the ribbon, we click on **Configure Site Components** and select **Software Update Point**.

3. On the initial screen that appears, we select the **Relevant** option for the software update point. Using this example as a guide, we need to select **Synchronize from Microsoft Update**.

4. Under the **Reporting Events** option, we also select **Do not create WSUS reporting events**.

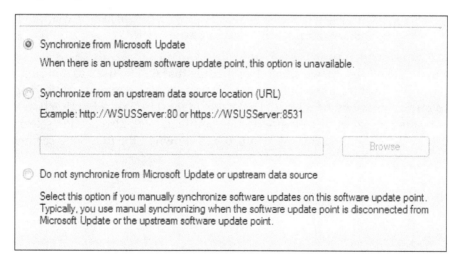

Next, we need to configure the classifications that are required; we need to select **Critical Updates** and **Security Updates** as shown in the following screenshot. These are the only two that are needed as per the requirements:

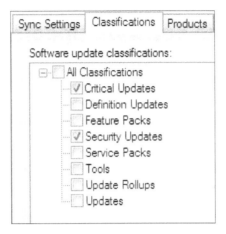

On the **Products** tab, we also need to select **Windows 8.1** and **Microsoft Office 2013**. **Windows 8.1** can be found under the **Windows** category and **Office 2013** under the **Office** category.

 For a new product to become available, you will have to wait until the initial synchronization has completed.

On the **Sync Schedule** tab, we select the schedule that will be used to determine when a full synchronization will take place. If you are also deploying definition updates for System Center Endpoint Protection, then this may determine how often you synchronize your software update point, and you also need to select the **Definition Updates on the classifications** tab as shown in the following screenshot:

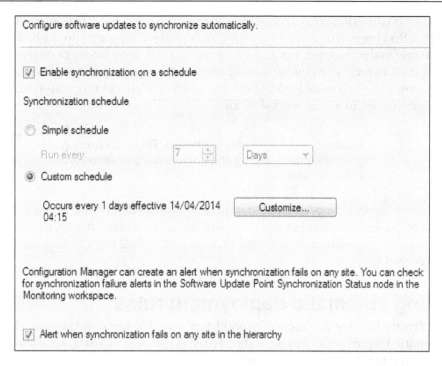

On the **Languages** tab, make sure you select the languages you need in your environment for your workstations.

Deploying patches to pilot devices

The deployment of patches is dependent on collections to determine where to deploy the updates to. Set up a collection to identify the pilot devices for workstation patching:

As you can see from the preceding screenshot, our collection has been given a meaningful name, and we have limited this collection to all of our Windows 7 workstations in this example. This limiting collection can prevent you from deploying things by mistake to devices that do not require the deployment.

Populate your collection with devices that require the patches to be deployed. As a good practice, users who have their devices in your pilot group should be a good mix of people in the business, not just everyone in your department or everyone in IT. Doing this ensures that you get a good mix of people who perform various roles; this way, you will get a good idea of how the patch will affect your wider estate when it is deployed to all the workstations.

 Make sure your pilot group is varied. This will ensure good coverage of your testing and prevent any problems further down the line.

When your collection has been created, you now need to determine which patches you want to deploy. For this example, we will use an automatic deployment rule. This will enable some automation of the process and reduce the administrative effort that is involved.

Creating automatic deployment rules

In the **Software Library** workspace, expand **Software Updates** and right-click on **Automatic Deployment Rules**. From here, you can select **Create Automatic Deployment Rule**. When the wizard opens, in the **General** tab, provide a name for the automatic deployment rule and select the collection you created with your pilot devices.

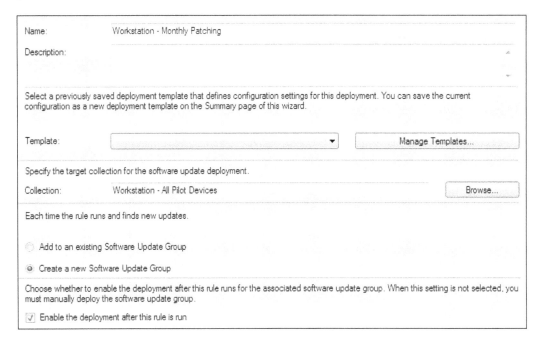

As you can see from the preceding screenshot, you need to also select **Create a new Software Update Group** and ensure that the checkbox is selected to enable the rule after the wizard has completed.

On the **Software Updates** page, check the two criteria, **Date Released or Revised** and **Update Classification**. In the criteria at the bottom of the screen, click on each item and enter the configuration as shown in the following screenshot:

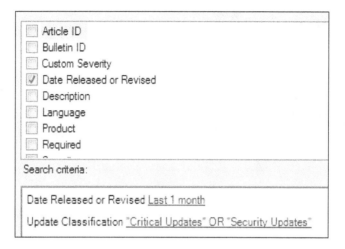

On the **Evaluation Schedule** page, we now need to configure the rule to run on the required schedule. Configure the schedule to run on every second Thursday of the month. This allows the clients to run a scan against the updates to see whether they are required or not and by which systems.

The default settings are used on the **Deployment Schedule**, **User Experience**, and **Alerts** pages as well as the **Download Settings** page.

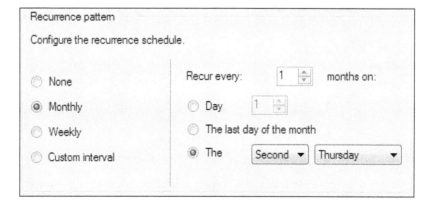

We set a new deployment package as per the preceding screenshot. From the **Sending priority** drop-down box, select **High**. Specify the distribution points that you want to distribute the content to. Run through the rest of the wizard and create the automatic deployment rule.

On a monthly basis, this will now distribute the latest monthly patches each month to our pilot collection of devices.

Deploying patches to live devices

When the time to deploy the updates to a live set of devices arrives, we again need another collection. As before, give the collection a meaningful name. In the membership rules, we can now exclude the collection of pilot devices. This just ensures that we do not deploy to the same devices twice—while this should not cause any problems, it is just a safety net.

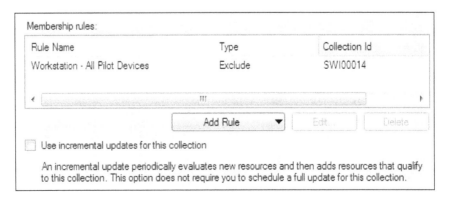

Now that you can see this collection in your collection list as before, you will see it along with the collection previously created for the pilot deployment.

Icon	Name	Limiting Collection
	Workstation - All Pilot Devices	All Windows 7 Workstations
	Workstation - Live Patching	All Windows 7 Workstations

As we told the automatic deployment rule to create a new software update group for each execution, we can use this to easily deploy the same group we deployed to the pilot collection, but this time, we deploy it to the live collection.

Right-click on the **Software Update** group and then select **Deploy**. As a good practice, provide a name that consists of the group you are deploying to and the month so you can identify it easily for reporting purposes.

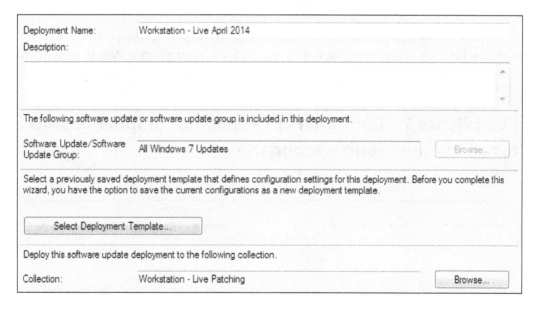

As before, accept the defaults on the remainder of the screens as we have already deployed the content and deployed this software update group using the automatic deployment rule.

Reporting patch compliance

As we have created a software update group with a monthly batch of updates, we can use this in a report to view the compliance of the software update group.

In the group **Software Updates – A Compliance**, you will see a report with the title **Compliance 1 – Overall compliance**. This report can be used to enter a software update group to view the overall compliance state for a specific collection against a software update group.

Compliance 1 - Overall compliance
⊞ Description

Collection Name ⇕	Clients in Collection ⇕
All Windows 7 Workstations	2

State ⇕	Count of Computers ⇕	% of Total ⇕
Compliance state unknown	2	100.00

This report shows you a count of the clients in the collection, followed by status messages for each compliance state; you can click on a compliance state to drill down to view more details. When you drill down on this report, you will see each machine that is listed in a specific compliance state as selected in the report parameters.

Compliance 7 - Computers in a specific compliance state for an update group (secondary)
⊞ Description

Device Name ⇕	Last Logged on User ⇕	Assigned Site ⇕	Client Version ⇕
		SWI	5.00.7958.1000
		SWI	5.00.7958.1000

You can view the compliance on a per update basis by running the report **Compliance 3 – Update** group (per update) in the same group as the previous report, which will show you the information on a per update level. This information is useful if you want to see the compliance of a software update group on a per update basis.

To obtain reports for a set of patches based on the quarter of a whole year, you can create another software update group that is used for reporting purposes. For yearly-based reporting, you can also run the report, **Compliance 4 – Updates by vendor month year**. This will show you a per update analysis of the compliance level for a specific collection.

If you want to view the compliance for the overall collection rather than per update, create a new software update baseline and report on the baseline using the **Compliance 1 – Overall compliance report**.

Obtaining compliance with a compliance baseline

Quite often in an organization, a security team or information security team will be the ones that instruct which patches should get deployed and which ones should not. With so many patches getting deployed for many different products, it can easily become confusing to determine your patch compliance.

You can use a community add-in for the console from The Desktop Team (`http://bit.ly/1nYpV5P`), which will allow you to create a compliance baseline from a software update group. This great utility is a superb addition to your arsenal of tools and will make the creation of your baseline simple.

When you have installed the add-in, simply right-click on a **Software Update** group and then select **Create Baseline** from the context menu, as shown in the following screenshot:

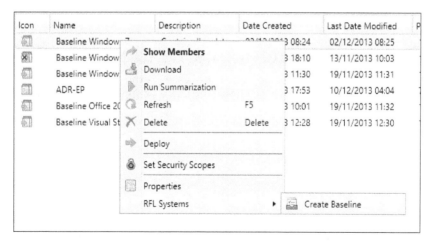

When your update baseline has been completed, you can run compliance reports on it.

A sample scenario to patch servers

Using the same example scenario and the same infrastructure, we will now look at patching for servers rather than workstations. As a review, here are the requirements from the customer.

Customer requirements

In this scenario, our customer will deploy patches to servers in a monthly cycle. This cycle will closely align with the Patch Tuesday concept.

- Deployments will be created and sent to a pilot group of workstations a week after the patches are released by Microsoft.

- Following the deployment of patches to a pilot group, the deployment will then be sent to the remainder of the workstations.

- Portions of the process need to be automated to reduce administrative effort.

- Only critical updates and security updates are required for Windows Server 2012 R2. No third-party or in-house updates are required.

- The solution needs to be implemented using existing equipment.

- The administrator should be able to report on patch compliance on either a monthly, quarterly, or yearly basis.

The organization has a simple Configuration Manager 2012 R2 hierarchy, with a single, standalone primary site that has 15,000 devices over two office locations. Both offices are well connected to the primary site, which is located in a managed data center by a third party.

Configuring maintenance windows

The deployment of the patches in terms of processes is the same for both workstations and servers; we do have some differences that we will need to address, though. The first one is how to control the deployment of our updates to servers.

This is done using maintenance windows, which are set at a collection level. A maintenance window defines when tasks can run; Configuration Manager will only run the updates if the maintenance window is long enough. For this reason, it is important that you give your servers plenty of time to apply appropriate updates.

Using the same principle for workstations with a pilot and live collection for the deployment of updates works really well for servers too. We use our pilot collection to make sure the patches do not cause any adverse problems that we will need to resolve.

Just like deploying updates to workstations, make sure your pilot collection contains low-risk servers over a cross section of your environment.

Applying maintenance windows to collections

Select the collection that you wish to apply to the maintenance window. Right-click and select **Properties** from the context menu or from the ribbon. In the **Properties** window, select the **Maintenance Windows** tab.

 As a best practice, it is recommended that you create separate collections to manage maintenance windows and use your main collections to target the deployment.

Enter a name in the maintenance window; this should be something you can easily identify so other people in your team can identify what has been set up:

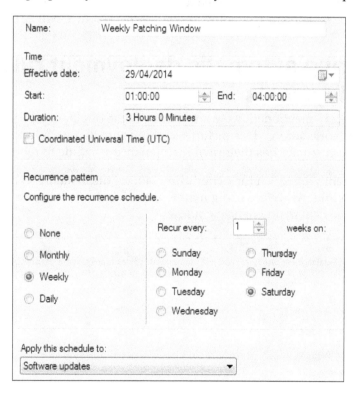

On your schedule, define how long you want the window to be and when the window will be effective from. In this example, we are using between 0100 and 0400 hours weekly on a Saturday. We also define that this maintenance window can only be used for software updates.

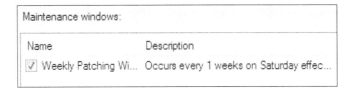

When you have created your maintenance window, you will see it listed in the tab in the collection properties.

If your server is part of multiple collections with two maintenance windows defined that overlap—for example, one maintenance window is 0100 to 0300 and another is 0230 to 0430—then the maintenance window for the specific resource will be 0100 to 0430.

Configuring automatic deployment rules and deployments

As we have already mentioned, we want to control the deployment of patches more than we do for workstations. This includes making sure that we suppress the reboots of servers as the customer has their own maintenance schedule to reboot servers.

In the deployment wizard, on the **Scheduling** tab, set the installation deadline to **As soon as possible**. As we are using maintenance windows, **As soon as possible**, in this case, is the next maintenance window:

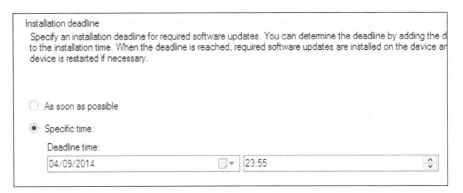

On the user experience screen in the deployment wizard, also make sure that the **Servers** checkbox is selected under the **Device restart behavior** section.

Summary

In this chapter, we explored how to implement patching for both workstations and servers. We discussed the importance of using pilot collections to ensure your environment is kept secure before deploying to the wider environment, and also looked at how to monitor your deployments and compliance using reporting and compliance baselines.

In the next chapter, we will have a look at reporting in Configuration Manager and how to create custom reports using Report Builder. We will also look at how to create charts using existing Configuration Manager data.

9
Advanced Reporting

Reporting in Configuration Manager 2012 has changed almost completely from its previous versions. The output, while informative, was criticized in Configuration Manager 2007; however, you could take advantage of reporting services in Configuration Manager 2007.

In Configuration Manager 2012, the reporting now takes full advantage of **SQL Reporting Services (SSRS)**. This means that your reports are more feature rich and the graphics you produce will be much more detailed.

In this chapter, we will follow a real-world reporting example from data that we are collecting as part of inventory and looking to expose in some custom reports in Configuration Manager. We will cover:

- An introduction to Report Builder
- Creating custom reports
- Creating custom charts
- Using report subscriptions

Report Builder

When you design a report, you specify where to get the data, what data to get, and how to display the data. When you run the report, the report processor takes all the information you have specified, retrieves the data, and combines it with the report layout to generate the report. You can preview your reports in Report Builder, or you can publish your report without looking at a preview.

Report Builder is a powerful tool that allows you to present the same dataset in formats, such as tables, charts, graphs, and maps when using geographic data.

Developing reports using Report Builder

The development of reports that are more detailed and available in different forms has become arguably harder than it used to be. Report Builder is a big subject that we certainly cannot cover in one chapter. A great supplement to this chapter would be a book dedicated to SSRS reporting that would cover the Report Builder functionality in much more detail, rather than a specific use case like we will cover in this chapter (`http://bit.ly/1vwHzVR`).

Requirements for reports

Any report that you create in Report Builder requires a minimum of two objects: the data source and the dataset. The data source is the object that defines connection information to the database and also provides any credentials if they are required.

The dataset contains the results of the query that has been executed against the data source. Each dataset contains a number of fields that are returned as defined in the SQL query or stored procedure.

To display data from the query, you need to add fields from a dataset onto the design canvas in Report Builder. This will then allow you to perform additional formatting of the data in terms of presentation and what is actually displayed.

Using Report Builder, you also have the ability to group and sort the data that is returned from the dataset using a wide range of parameters and options.

Configuring Report Builder for Configuration Manager

Before you start developing reports using Report Builder on a remote machine, you will need the SQL Server certificate from the server. In case this certificate is not imported, you will get the following message using Report Builder when you attempt to connect to the data source:

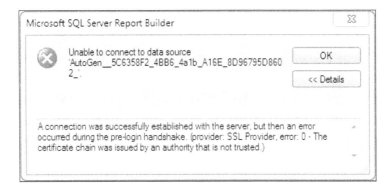

You can resolve this error message by importing a certificate from the database server, which may also be your primary site or central administration site. Using the certificates snap-in for MMC, connect to the local computer certificate store. In the **Personal certificate** store, you should see a certificate like the one shown in the following screenshot:

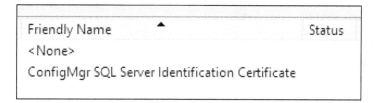

Export the certificate with the **ConfigMgr SQL Server Identification Certificate** friendly name, as highlighted, without the private key. Once the certificate has been exported, import it on the machine that you wish to run Report Builder on. The certificate should be placed in the **Trusted Root** store in the local computer section.

Creating custom reports

In order to create custom reports, you need to know where the data is stored. When retrieving data from Configuration Manager, you should also use the views that are provided rather than the raw data stored in tables.

To help assist with the design of the reports, Microsoft has published information on the schema of the database, including the documentation on the various views in the database (http://bit.ly/PNqkfg). This information will help you find the information that you need, should it not be available.

Defining the report requirements

In this reporting example, we will be creating a report off a custom inventory that has been collected by Configuration Manager. The data is information from the registry about what version of the operating system build is used in the estate. In this example, we will create two reports; the first report will show all the machines with a specific build version, and the second report will show a count of all the machines running all versions of the existing build.

The first report will be called **All machines with a specific build version**; we will provide a parameter that is a drop-down box that lists all the version numbers that exist in the database from inventoried machines. The report will then show the NetBIOS name of the computer, along with the version number and deployment time from the database. This is information that is collected from the client when the inventory takes place. The report will drill down to the built-in report computer information for a specific computer.

The second report will show each version number, along with a count of how many clients are running the specified version; the report will drill down by clicking a version number taking the viewer of the report to the first report that we are creating so they can see which machines are running this version. This report will be called **Count of all machines running all build versions**.

Creating the initial report layout

When you run a built-in report from Configuration Manager, you will notice that the format and style of the reports is consistent. Depending on your requirements, you can create your report to match the style of the other built-in reports or your own corporate style.

For this example, we are using a template that has been created by saving an existing report. This template is based on the existing built-in design with the blue header and the Configuration Manager logo in the top-right corner. Be careful to strip out any references to an old report or you will not be able to save the report.

 Using a template gives your reports a consistent style and saves time during the design phase of your custom report. You can replace the image with your own by overwriting the default logo.

Adding the data source to the report

When you have your new report saved, on the left-hand side pane of the **Report Builder** screen, right-click on **Data Sources** and add a new data source. Provide a name for the new data source and browse to the existing data source on your Configuration Manager reporting server, as shown in the following screenshot:

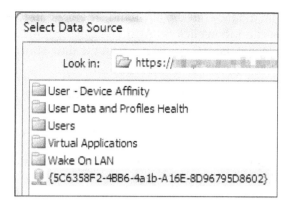

When you have configured the preceding options, you should see a similar configuration to the one shown as follows. When you are happy with the configuration, click on **OK** to close the window and save the data source.

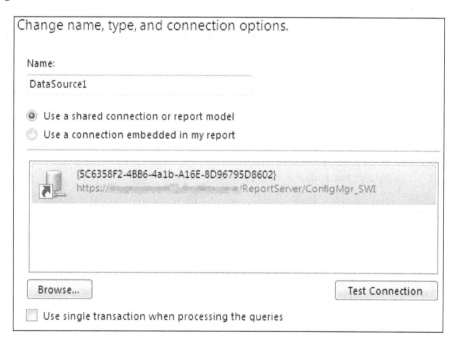

Creating the first report

The first report that we are creating is the one titled **All machines with a specific build version**. In order to provide the parameter for the main query to discover the machines with a specific build version, we need to provide a query that will show all the possible options for the parameter.

This is done by creating a dataset in the left-hand side pane in **Report Builder**. Right-click on **Datasets** and then click on **Add Dataset**. Provide a name for the dataset; in this example, we use `DS_Values`. Select the data source that you created and then enter the following query:

```
SELECT dbo.v_GS_BuildData0.BuildVersion0 FROM dbo.v_GS_BuildData0
UNION
SELECT dbo.v_GS_BuildData640.BuildVersion0 FROM dbo.v_GS_BuildData640
```

As the information is registry based, the views contain information for both 32-bit and 64-bit registry locations. The **BuildVersion0** column in the database view, which contains the version number, is the one we need.

Using the union keyword in SQL, we are able to run the select query on both views in the database against the column, **BuildVersion0**; the keyword will remove any duplicate version numbers from the results that are returned and leave us with a list that contains only unique version numbers.

This information can then be used as our dataset for the parameter. When you have entered this query into **Dataset Properties**, you should have a screen that looks similar to the following one:

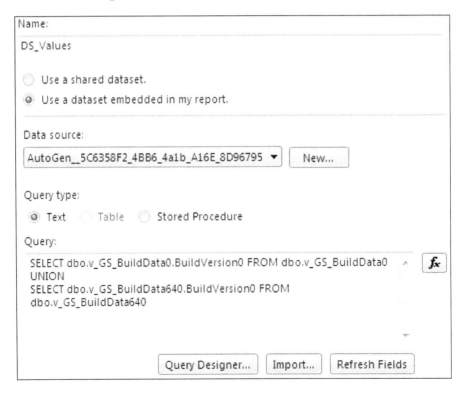

You can click on the **Query Designer** button to test the results of the query quickly to make sure the data returned is what you expect. No other options are required in the dataset properties. From here, once you are satisfied with the setup, you can click on **OK** to close the window.

Creating the parameter for the report

Now, we need to create another dataset; this dataset will be used to obtain the actual query results based on the version number that we specify in the parameter. Before we create this second dataset, we need to create a parameter. In the left-hand side pane in **Report Builder**, right-click on **Parameters** and select **Add Parameter**.

In the **Name** field, enter BuildVersion (note that this does not have any spaces). Then in the **Prompt** field, enter Build Version (note that this does have spaces). As our report will not generate any information without a parameter value, ensure that the following options are not checked:

- **Allow blank value**
- **Allow null value**
- **Allow multiple values**

When these options have been configured, click on the **Available Values** tab on the left-hand side of the window. Select the radio button, **Get values from a query**. Select the previous dataset that was created, and then set the value and label fields to **BuildVersion0**. You should now have this tab configured, as shown in the following screenshot:

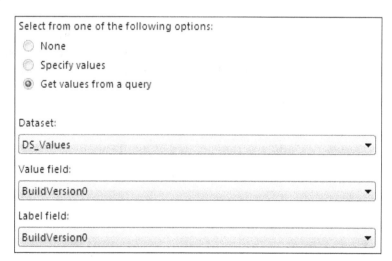

Click on the **General** tab and ensure your parameter configuration matches the following screenshot:

Creating the results dataset

When our parameter has been created, we can now use this parameter in the second dataset we need to create. We create another dataset and point it to the same data source we created earlier.

This time, the query is a little more complicated; it still uses a union keyword to ensure that we remove any duplicate entries. However, this time, we use a `join` statement to retrieve the NetBIOS name of the resource from the `v_GS_SYSTEM` view. We do this by running the `join` statement on the resource ID column of the `v_GS_BuildData` and `v_GS_SYSTEM` views to obtain the **Name0** column from this view.

Before we place the query into the query window, we click on the **Parameters** tab in the dataset properties. We add a parameter and enter the name as `@BuildVersion` (the symbol is the control character for a parameter in SQL). In the value, we enter the following by clicking on the function button:

```
=Parameters!BuildVersion.Value
```

The **Parameters** tab should now look like the following screenshot:

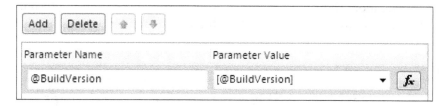

The function window should then look like the following screenshot. This is the function that will define the value that is passed, so it is important that it is typed correctly:

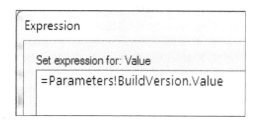

Go back to the **Query** tab in the dataset properties. Enter the following SQL query in the box provided. Note that we have included the parameter that we just created. You can see this highlighted in the following query:

```
SELECT v_GS_SYSTEM.Name0, v_GS_BuildData640.BuildVersion0, v_GS_
BuildData640.DeploymentTimeStamp0
FROM v_GS_SYSTEM INNER JOIN
v_GS_BuildData640 ON v_GS_SYSTEM.ResourceID = v_GS_BuildData640.
ResourceID WHERE v_GS_BuildData640.BuildVersion0 = @BuildVersion
UNION
SELECT v_GS_SYSTEM.Name0, v_GS_BuildData0.BuildVersion0, v_GS_
BuildData0.DeploymentTimeStamp0
FROM v_GS_SYSTEM INNER JOIN
v_GS_BuildData0 ON v_GS_SYSTEM.ResourceID = v_GS_BuildData0.ResourceID
WHERE v_GS_BuildData0.BuildVersion0 = @BuildVersion
```

No other configuration is required here; you can now click on **OK** to save the dataset.

Formatting and displaying the data

In your template there should be a tabix control, which allows you to present data from a dataset. You can see the tabix highlighted in the following screenshot from the finished report:

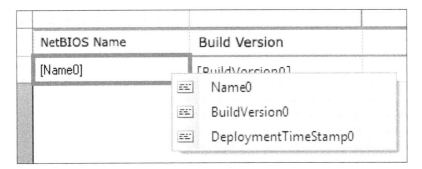

Your report will contain three columns: the first is the NetBIOS name of the computer, the second is the version number of the deployment, and the final column is a timestamp that shows when the deployment finished. Enter these titles at the top in the bold section of the tabix.

To display the values, select the cell where you want to display the data, click on the button that appears on the right-hand side of the screen, and select the data you wish to display in that cell. You can see this in the following screenshot:

As our NetBIOS column will also link to another report, it needs configuring too. Right-click on the textbox for the NetBIOS column and click on the **Action** tab. Select **Go to report** and then select the report, **Computer information for a specific computer**; this can be found in the **Hardware – General** category.

Add the parameter at the bottom of the report and select **Variable** as the name and then **[Name0]** as the value. Your configuration for this tab should look like the following screenshot:

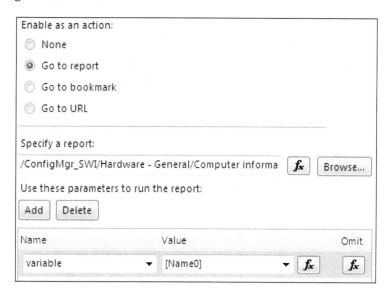

Normally, hyperlinks have different styling, so the viewer can easily determine that a portion of text is a hyperlink. Report Builder does not do this for you. For this reason, you need to change the style of the text. If you are using Configuration Manager styled reports, then you will notice that they just underline the text to show a hyperlink.

Now, click on **Run** in the top-left corner of **Report Builder**. You will be presented with the parameter that we created, and your values should be the ones you have from your inventory. It should look like the following screenshot:

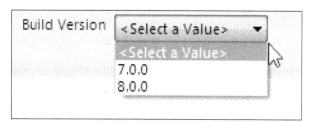

Select a value and then click on **View Report**. This will execute the report and look for the results based on the version you have selected in the parameter. Provided you have data in your database, you should have something like the following screenshot:

All machines with a specific build version
⊞ Description

NetBIOS Name	⇅	Build Version	⇅	Deployment Time	⇅
		7.0.0		16/04/2014 08:08:44	

Test the hyperlink by clicking on the report. This should take you to the linked report so you can see more information about the computer. Once you have confirmed this is working as expected, your report will be complete. Save your report so it can be accessed via the reporting node.

Creating the second report

The second report that we are creating will show a count of the machines that are running the build versions. This report is much simpler to build than the first one and only requires one dataset to produce the information we need.

We will also be using the formatting options from within Report Builder and the functionality of the expression engine to display the count of machines.

Creating the dataset for the report

Create a new dataset and select the data source, which should be set up first. The same process that was used earlier will be used here. In the query box, enter the following query; this is the same query as one of the commands used earlier:

```
SELECT dbo.v_GS_BuildData0.BuildVersion0 FROM dbo.v_GS_BuildData0
UNION
SELECT dbo.v_GS_BuildData640.BuildVersion0 FROM dbo.v_GS_BuildData640
```

No additional configuration is required for this dataset, so make sure your configuration matches the one shown as follows and then click on **OK** to save and create the dataset when you are satisfied with it:

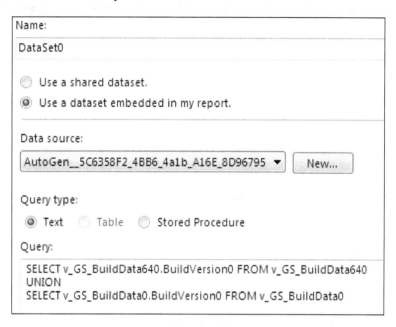

Once the dataset has been created, configure the tabix so that we have the header's build version and count. Select the build version field, right-click on the textbox, and select **Expression**.

Enter the expression in the box provided. Your expression field should look like the next screenshot. Here is the expression in text form—`=Count(Fields!BuildVersion0.Value)`:

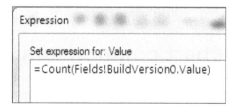

Again, this report will contain a link to the first report that we created; as before, right-click on the textbox for the build version count and select **Properties**. Link the field to another report that in this case is the first report we just created. Pass the **BuildVersion0** field as the parameter value. You can see this configuration in the following screenshot:

Creating custom charts

Report Builder also contains the ability to add charts known as data visualizations. This is a really powerful way of displaying textual data. For example, if you have a geographic dataset, you could present the data in textual format as well as a map.

A number of data visualization components are available within Report Builder. The charts that are available are very similar to those available in Microsoft Excel within Office. You can also add a gauge to the canvas, a map, data bar, and sparkline, as well as red, amber, and green indicators.

Working with chart components

Chart components can be added by clicking on a component from the **Insert** menu on the ribbon. In this example, we will use the dataset from the second report that we created to add a bar chart.

Select **Chart** wizard from the drop-down menu on the ribbon; then, select the existing dataset we created in the previous section. Select the chart type as a column chart. Drag **BuildVersion0** into the **Values** box and select the count aggregation from the drop-down menu on the right-hand side of the object. Also, drag **BuildVersion0** into the **Series** field.

Select a style for the chart depending on your requirements. When you click on **Finish**, you will see the graph on the report, as shown in the following screenshot:

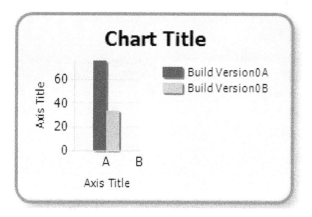

Configuring data visualizations

When you enter your chart on the canvas, you can edit the component as you did in Excel. You can change the style of the component as well as the properties of the data and data values without having to run through the wizard again.

When you click on the chart, you will see the **Chart Data** pop-up menu appear on the right-hand side of the chart on the screen:

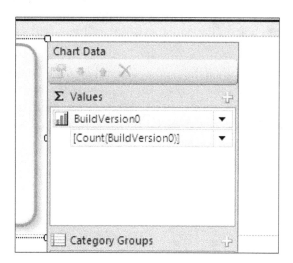

It is in this pop-up menu that you can begin to edit the values, categories, and series in the report.

Optimizing query performance

Query performance is an important part of the performance of reporting services. The majority of slow performance problems when working with reporting are slow-performing queries.

If you are querying large amounts of data, run your query through Database Engine Tuning Advisor with SQL Management Studio to see whether any improvements can be made. This is highly recommended if you are executing your own queries against the database. It will ensure the health of the database is maintained and the response times are as accurate as possible.

Configuring report subscriptions

A report subscription in Reporting Services is a recurring request to deliver a report at a specific time or in response to an event, and in an application, it is the file format that you specify in the subscription. Subscriptions provide an alternative to running a report on demand. On-demand reporting requires that you actively select the report each time you want to view it. In contrast, subscriptions can be used to schedule and then automate the delivery of a report.

Creating report subscriptions

Report subscriptions can be created from within Configuration Manager. In the **Monitoring** workspace, click on a report from within one of the reporting categories on the ribbon, or right-click on the context menu, and you will see the **Create Subscription** option.

On the subscription wizard, by default, you can only deliver the report to a Windows file share. You can enable the e-mail delivery of a report by configuring the e-mail options within the reporting services instance. More information on how to configure e-mail delivery can be found in SQL Server TechNet Library at `http://bit.ly/1jdbmLi`.

For file share delivery, you can deliver the report in a number of ways. They are as follows:

- XML
- CSV
- TIFF
- PDF
- HTML
- MHTML

- RPL Renderer
- Excel
- Word

You also have the ability to set up overwrite options for the report and it can run on a schedule as well. The following screenshot shows an example setup of the initial screen of the subscription wizard:

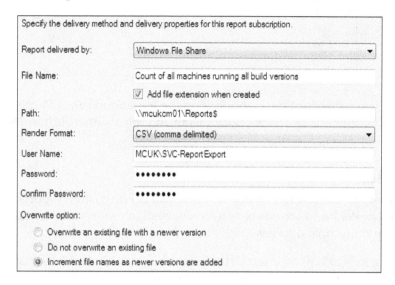

When you have defined the settings for the subscription, you can specify the schedule for the report. In this example, we will run the schedule daily between Monday and Friday. It is important to note that the schedule time is local to the SRS server, not the Configuration Manager site. If you work in multiple time zones, make sure you take this into account:

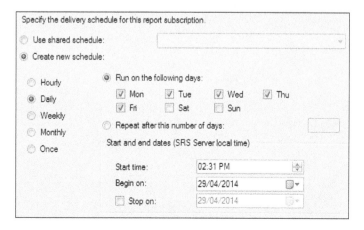

When the schedule has been created, if the report has parameters, you need to provide the parameters on the next screen. When this is done, you can create the subscription:

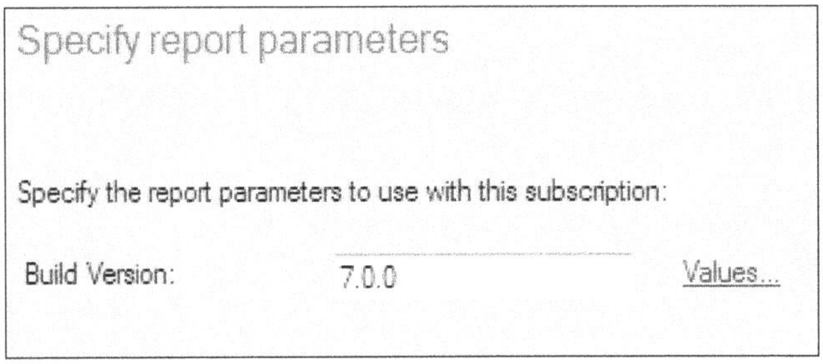

Specify report parameters

Specify the report parameters to use with this subscription:

Build Version: 7.0.0 Values...

To edit or delete a subscription, right-click on the report and select **Properties**. Then, select the subscription in the **Subscriptions** tab and select either **Edit** or **Delete**.

Summary

In this chapter, we took a high-level tour of how to create custom reports using Report Builder. We had a look at how to create custom reports that contain parameters and multiple datasets.

We also had a look at how to insert data visualizations, such as charts, to our reports and customize them to add our own data and customize the look and feel of the chart.

In the next chapter, we will have a look at how to prevent a configuration drift in our environment for our own internal processes and regulatory requirements. We will also look at using Configuration Manager to remediate configuration drift issues as well as report on them.

10
Preventing Configuration Drift

In any organization, large or small, at some point in the life cycle of a workstation or server, the problem of configuration drift is likely to arise. It is important to understand that the monitoring and, ultimately, the remediation of the desired state of the state configuration will improve the reliability of a system and increase its security and performance.

Configuration Manager allows administrators to configure baseline settings in functionality known as **Compliance Settings**. In previous versions of Configuration Manager, this was known as **Desired Configuration Management (DCM)**.

In this chapter, we will explore when to use compliance settings, how to use them to monitor for regulatory compliance, and how to remediate configuration drift from within Configuration Manager. We will cover the following topics:

- An introduction to compliance settings
- When to use compliance settings
- Example scenarios for compliance monitoring
- Remediating configuration drift

An introduction to compliance settings

Compliance settings contains tools to help you assess the compliance of devices and users for many different configurations, such as whether the correct operating system is installed and configured appropriately, whether all required applications are installed and configured correctly, whether optional applications are configured appropriately, and whether any prohibited applications are installed. Additionally, you can check for compliance using any of the following:

- Software updates
- Security settings
- Mobile devices

Configuration item settings using any of the following types can be automatically remediated when noncompliant settings are found:

- **Windows Management Instrumentation (WMI)**
- Registry
- Script
- All mobile device settings

> The majority of WMI settings are read only, so you are unlikely to be able to remediate the majority of the WMI settings.

Clients evaluate their compliance against deployed baselines and report the status back to the site using state and status messages. If the client is not on the network when the evaluation takes place, the results are then sent on reconnection. Administrators can monitor the results from within the **Deployments** node in the **Monitoring** workspace. You can also run reports to view more information about the compliance state of clients.

Use cases for compliance settings

You can use compliance settings for any number of reasons. Some of the most common reasons for organizations to implement compliance settings are as follows:

- To monitor the configuration of specific software against best practices from the software vendor
- To identify unauthorized changes in the configuration of servers
- To report compliance against regulatory and in-house policies
- To automatically remediate noncompliant settings where applicable
- To remediate compliance by deploying additional applications or packages

In this chapter, we will explore the setup of some of the preceding listed scenarios.

 The limitations to what you can do with compliance settings are really down to your imagination. Use compliance settings to ensure your environment is secure, stable, and performing in top condition.

Remedying of noncompliant clients

Configuration Manager supports the remediation of noncompliant clients where they have reported that a specific configuration item is not reporting as compliant. Configuration Manager supports the automatic remediation of the following configuration settings:

- WMI
- Registry
- Scripts
- Mobile device settings

You can only remediate mobile device settings when the mobile device in question is enrolled by Configuration Manager.

Example scenarios for compliance monitoring

In this section, we are going to look at some examples of where we would monitor compliance and run through the process of setting this up in the console and deploying the baseline to a collection.

We will explore the setup and configuration for the following scenarios:

- Monitoring the configuration settings of a specific application
- Monitoring for unauthorized software applications on servers

Monitoring application-specific settings

In this example, we will create some compliance items for software called Snowdrop. The monitoring will come in two configuration items. The first item will monitor a registry key to ensure the correct license key is in the registry, and the second configuration item will monitor for a specific file that contains some application settings.

In order for the application to function properly, both the registry key and the file must be in place. Our customer has also asked that we provide automatic remediation should the compliance check return a noncompliance. The registry key needs to be changed to the corporate site license, and the configuration file needs to be copied down from the master source.

Creating the configuration item

For this baseline, we will monitor two items. The first item will look at the registry key and the second one will look at the configuration file. We can place both of the configuration items together; however, later on we will learn how to remediate the presence of the configuration file. For reporting purposes, I believe it is a good idea to separate out the configuration items, especially when you are performing remediation, because Configuration Manager cannot automatically remediate all of the configuration items.

 Configuration Manager can only automatically remediate the following configuration items: WMI, registry, scripts, and mobile device settings.

In the **Assets and Compliance** workspace, expand **Compliance settings** and click on the **Configuration Items** node. If you are deploying lots of compliance items, then as a best practice, organize them into folders. The structure of this is down to your individual requirements.

 You must have detection and remediation rules that match; for example, you cannot detect a registry setting and have a script for the remediation.

From the ribbon or by right-clicking on the node, select **Create Configuration Item**, as shown in the following screenshot:

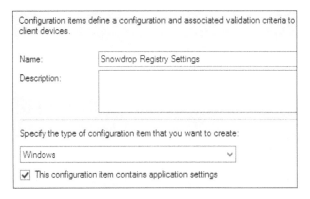

As seen from the preceding screenshot, we have provided a name for our configuration item as well as ticked the **This configuration item contains application settings** checkbox.

When this box is ticked, an additional option, **Detection methods**, is enabled in the wizard. This is important because we only want to validate the settings in this configuration item if the application is installed or the results we get are skewed.

As we deploy this application via Configuration Manager on the **Detection methods** tab in the wizard, we can select the **Detect a specific application and deployment type** option, as shown in the following screenshot:

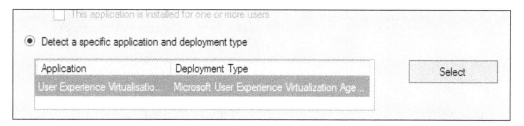

Click on **Select**, and then from the window, select the application and deployment type you wish to use; then, click on **OK**. You can also use a script to perform the detection as well as specify an MSI file for the detection.

When you click on **Next**, you can specify the settings for the configuration item. Create a new item and proceed to enter the values for your configuration item:

Name:	License Key Validation
Description:	Valiates the license key for Snowdrop is correct.
Setting type:	Registry value
Data type:	String

Specify the registry value to assess for compliance on computers.

Hive Name:	HKEY_LOCAL_MACHINE
Key Name:	SOFTWARE\Snowdrop
Value Name:	LicenseKey

☐ This registry value is associated with a 64-bit application

From the preceding screenshot, you can see that we have added a new registry value; we are looking for a string data type, and we have specified that we would like to look in HKEY_LOCAL_MACHINE. We then look in SOFTWARE\Snowdrop. The value we want to look for is called LicenseKey.

Notice the checkbox that says the key is associated with a 64-bit application. This ensures that Configuration Manager looks in the correct place in the registry if applicable. Ensure the setting for this box is correct to avoid unexpected results.

On the **Compliance rules** tab, we also created a new setting that will be used as the validation. We are looking for a specific value to be returned in the key, which is our license key:

You can also see that we checked the options to ensure that if this rule reports back as noncompliant, we want this remediating. This will be done by Configuration Manager automatically.

 Automatic remediation doesn't mean remediating as an administrator; it is a great piece of automation that can help improve your clients.

When you have set up the rule and validation settings, make sure you select the platforms this runs on. Like operating system deployment, it is important to ensure you only run this on the correct platforms.

This configuration item is now created—as we have already mentioned, we are going to create another configuration item for the configuration file. Create a new configuration item, as discussed in the preceding section, up to the step where we created the setting.

In this instance, create a new setting as follows:

- **Name: Configuration File**
- **Setting type: File system**
- **Type: File**

You can see the other settings that we have used in the following screenshot of the configuration screen:

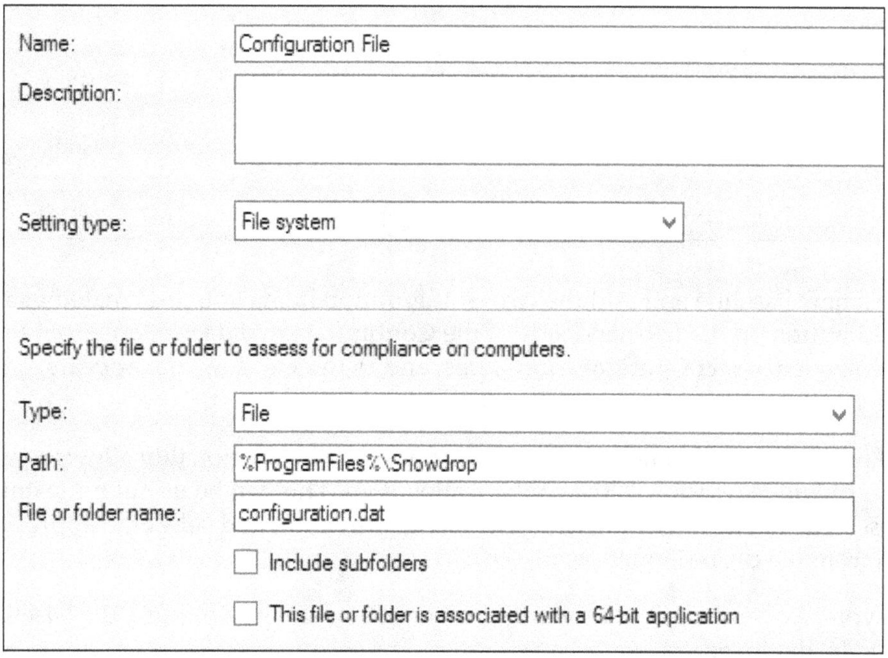

To provide the file path, we should use variables where possible. This will ensure it works on as many different configurations as possible. You can use the **Browse** button as well to connect to another machine and browse the filesystem. As with the previous setting, ensure you check the box if required when looking at 64-bit applications.

The compliance rule for this setting is really simple. We just want to make sure it exists. Create a new compliance rule and change the rule type to existential. Leave the default checkbox at the bottom of the screen that states **File must exist on client devices**.

Creating the configuration baseline

When the configuration items have been created, before we can deploy them to a client, we need to add them to a baseline:

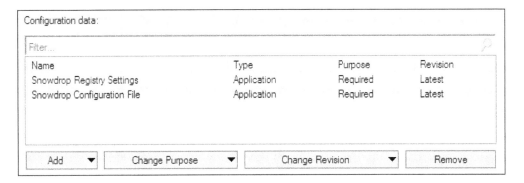

Create a new baseline and add the two configuration items you just created using the **Add** button on the left-hand side of the **Configuration data** section. From the drop-down list, select **Configuration items**, and in the window that appears, one by one select the items you created.

By default, the **Revision** field will be set to **Latest**. This functionality allows you to use a previous revision of the configuration item. This can be useful for testing purposes, for example. Simply click on **Change Revision** and select the appropriate option from the drop-down box.

When you have added all of the configuration items that you require, the baseline is ready to be deployed.

Deploying the configuration baseline

Configuration baselines are deployed to collections such as other objects in Configuration Manager. Right-click on the baseline you wish to deploy and select **Deploy** from the context menu, as shown in the following screenshot:

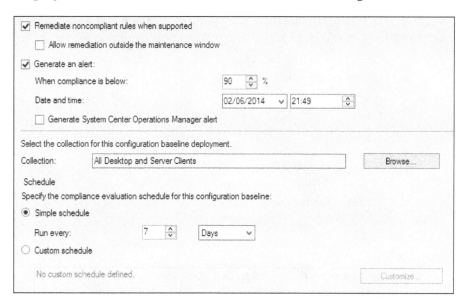

As you can see from the preceding screenshot, we have a few options. The first is a checkbox that allows us to remediate any rules that are noncompliant. We can also generate alerts in the console when the percentage compliance falls below a specified level.

 You need to check the box in the deployment that states that noncompliant rules should be remediated when supported, otherwise this functionality will not work.

We can also configure integration with the Operations Manager agent if it is installed; an alert will be generated, if required, when the box is checked. Finally, select a collection to deploy the baseline to and specify a schedule. What you specify in this section will determine how often the rule is run by the Configuration Manager agent.

When you have verified all the settings are correct, click on **OK** to create the deployment.

Monitoring the deployment

The very basic monitoring of a baseline deployment can be performed via the **Deployment** tab on the baseline settings. You will see the overall percentage compliance against a specific collection at a basic level.

For more detailed information, you can view the deployment in the **Deployments** tab in the **Monitoring** workspace or leverage the reports available for reporting.

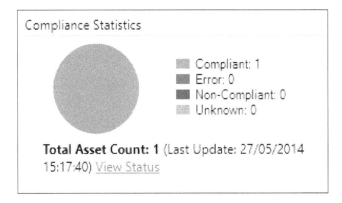

In the preceding figure, you will see a detailed pie chart that shows the number of clients that are in a **Compliant**, **Error**, **Non-Compliant**, or **Unknown** state. Click on **View Status** to find out more information about the clients in a specific state.

Clicking on each of the states at the top of the detail will show you information about the specific configuration items, and then by clicking on the configuration item, you will see the clients that have reported in that specific state.

In the reporting node, as an administrator, you also have 17 reports available to you. These reports can view information all the way from high-level to much more detailed reports if you require them.

Remediating the file presence

When we want to remediate a configuration item that cannot be remediated automatically by Configuration Manager, it does not mean that it isn't possible. From the active deployment, you can right-click on **Deployment** and select **Create New Collection**, as shown in the following screenshot:

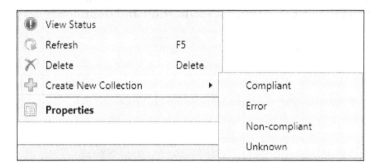

Click on **Non-compliant** in the context menu, and a new, query-based collection will be created that contains all the computers that are noncompliant for the selected baseline. When the collection has been created, you can then deploy a package or application depending on your requirements to resolve the failed compliance.

In this instance, to resolve our problem with the configuration file for our application, we could simply create a package that will copy the file from a master source on the network to the correct directory locally.

The next time the client runs a compliance check and reports back as compliant, the membership will be updated and the client will drop out of the collection on the next collection update.

Monitoring unauthorized software applications

Another common use for compliance settings would be to detect applications that seem unauthorized. A great place to use this functionality would be on servers, which often require a very specific configuration.

In this example, we will create a configuration item that will detect the presence of an application that we do not want installed on our servers. We will then remediate any noncompliant servers using compliance settings.

Creating the configuration item

The application we want to detect is the UE-V client. As before, we create a new compliance item and check the box to say this configuration setting contains application settings that will enable the detection method option in the wizard.

As before, this is an application we are deploying via Configuration Manager, so we can select it using the **Detect a specific application and deployment type** option:

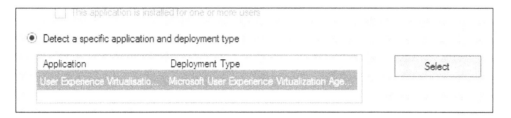

At this point, unless you require more specific settings, you can skip through the rest of the wizard and create the configuration item. As before, make sure that you select the platforms you wish to deploy this configuration item to. As we are using this to remove software, it is important that it is properly set.

Creating the configuration baseline

Create a new configuration baseline and add in the configuration item for the software detection that we just created. Select the configuration item and click on **Change Purpose**. Select **Prohibited** from the drop-down list as shown in the following screenshot:

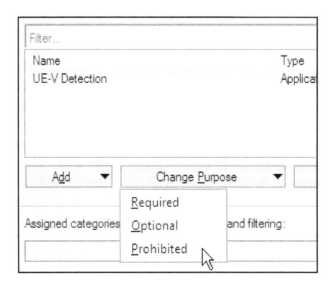

Once **Prohibited** is selected, this should be reflected in the configuration data section of the baseline settings. This is an important setting in the overall setup of this process. You can see the updated screen in the following screenshot:

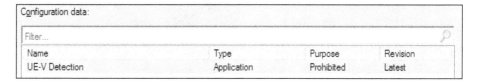

Removing the software where it is detected

In this example, we cannot allow Configuration Manager to automatically remediate this configuration item as it is not supported. In this example, we need to create a new collection of noncompliant clients.

Right-click on the collection in the **Deployments** tab, select **Create New Collection**, and then select **Non-compliant**, as shown in the following screenshot:

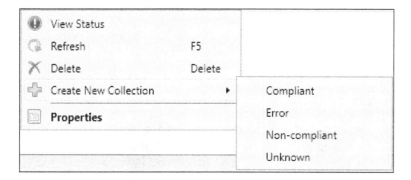

When the collection has been created, we can create a new deployment for the application, which already exists in Configuration Manager. For this to work properly, the uninstall string must be populated in the application configuration.

In the deployment settings, make sure, as per the following screenshot, that you have selected **Action** as **Uninstall**:

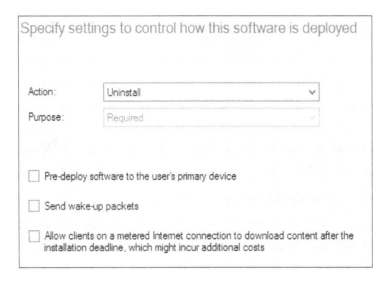

When this is deployed out to the collection, which is populated with servers that have UE-V installed, it will be uninstalled automatically.

Summary

In this chapter, we explored how to use compliance settings to your advantage to manage your environment. The key to using compliance settings in your environment is to plan what you want to do. As you have seen, you can monitor a wide range of settings, which means the only limit to what you can monitor and remediate depends on what you want to do.

In the next chapter, we will take a look at how to use Configuration Manager to begin managing our own device. We will take a look at how to manage and deploy company resources as well as look at the use of Exchange Connector and Windows Intune, both of which can be used in Configuration Manager.

11
Managing Bring Your Own Device and Mobility

One of the biggest subjects in technology is the way IT organizations manage bring your own device and mobility. The subject can include forms such as choose your own device, buy your own device, and many other forms. One thing that is common in any scheme is that as an organization, our IT departments need to adapt to and evolve in the way our users work.

Configuration Manager contains a number of tools that extend your management capabilities for devices that the user either owns or rents from the company. In this chapter, we will explore some of these options and look at how they can help you manage mobility in your workforce. We'll cover the following topics:

- Deploying company resource profiles
- Managing roaming devices
- Integrating the Microsoft Exchange connector
- Using Windows Intune

Deploying company resource profiles

One of the improvements that shipped with the R2 release of Configuration Manager 2012 was the ability to deploy company resources such as Wi-Fi profiles, certificates, and VPN profiles. This functionality really opened up the management story for organizations that already have a big take up of bring your own device or have mobility in their long-term strategy.

 You do not need Windows Intune to deploy company resource profiles.

The company resource profiles are really useful in extending some of the services that you provide to domain-based clients using Group Policy. Some examples of this include deploying VPN and Wi-Fi profiles to domain clients using Group Policy preferences.

As you cannot deploy a group policy to non-domain-joined devices, it becomes really useful to manage and deploy these via Configuration Manager.

Another great use case for company resource profiles is deploying certificates. Configuration Manager includes the functionality to allow managed clients to have certificates enrolled to them. This can include those resources that rarely or never contact the domain. This scenario is becoming more common, so it is important that we have the capability to deploy these settings to users without relying on the domain.

Managing Wi-Fi profiles with Configuration Manager

The deployment of Wi-Fi profiles in Configuration Manager is very similar to that of a manual setup. The wizard provides you with the same options that you would expect to see should you configure the network manually within Windows.

You can also configure a number of security settings, such as certificates for clients and server authentication. You can configure the following device types with Wi-Fi profiles:

- Windows 8.1 32-bit
- Windows 8.1 64-bit
- Windows RT 8.1
- Windows Phone 8.1
- iOS 5, iOS 6, and iOS 7
- iOS 5, iOS 6, and iOS 7
- Android devices that run Version 4

Configuring a Wi-Fi network profile in Configuration Manager is a simple process that is wizard-driven. First, in the **Assets and Compliance** workspace, expand **Compliance Settings** and **Company Resource Access**, and then click on **Wi-Fi Profiles**. Right-click on the node and select **Create Wi-Fi Profile**, or select this option from the home tab on the ribbon.

Specify general information about this Wi-Fi profile

Name: Contoso_Corp|

Description:

☐ Import an existing Wi-Fi profile item from a file

On the general page of the wizard, provide a name for the profile. If required, you can add a description here as well. If you have exported the settings from a Windows 8.1 device, you can import them here as well.

Specify general information about this Wi-Fi profile

Network name: Contoso

SSID: Contoso_Corp

☑ Connect automatically when this network is in range

☐ Look for other wireless networks while connected to this network

☐ Connect when the network is not broadcasting its name (SSID)

Click on **Next** in the **Wi-Fi Profile** page that you need to provide information about the network you want to connect to. **Network Name** is what is displayed on the users' device and so should be friendly for them. You also need to enter the SSID of the network. Make sure this is entered correctly as clients will use this to attempt to connect to the network.

You can also specify other settings here, like you can in Windows, such as specifying whether we should connect if the network is not broadcasting or while the network is in range. Click on **Next** to continue to the security configuration page.

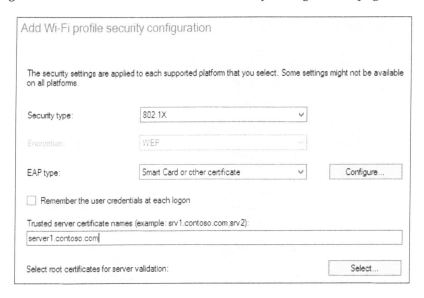

Depending on the security, encryption, and **Extensible Authentication Protocol** (**EAP**) settings that you select, some items on this page of the wizard might not be available. As shown in the previous screenshot, the settings you configure here replicate those that you can configure in Windows when manually connecting to the network.

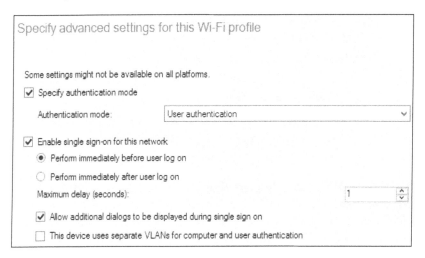

On the **Advanced Settings** page of **Create Wi-Fi Profile Wizard**, specify any additional settings for the Wi-Fi profile. This can be the authentication mode, single sign-on options, and **Federal Information Processing Standards (FIPS)** compliance.

If you require any proxy settings, you can also configure these on the next page as well as providing information on which platforms should process this profile. When the profile has been created, you can then right-click on the profile to deploy it to a collection.

Managing certificates with Configuration Manager

Deploying a certificate profile in Configuration Manager is actually a little quicker than creating a Wi-Fi profile. However, before you move on to deploying a certificate, you need some prerequisites in your environment.

First, you need to deploy the **Network Device Enrollment Service (NDES)**, which is part of the Certificate Services functionality in Windows Server. You can find guidance on deploying NDES in the Active Directory TechNet library at `http://bit.ly/1kjpgxD`.

You must then install and configure at least one certificate registration point in the Configuration Manager hierarchy, and you can install this site system role in the central administration site or in a primary site.

Specify the certificate registration point settings

A certificate registration point communicates with a server that runs the Network Device Enrollment Service to manage device certificate requests that use the Simple Certificate Enrollment Protocol (SCEP).

Website name:	Default Web Site	HTTPS port number: 443
Virtual application name:	CMCertificateRegistration	

Specify the servers that run the Network Device Enrollment Service. These servers must be configured with a PKI client authentication certificate. For Configuration Manager to validate this certificate, you must specify the root certificate for the issuing certification authority (CA).

URL for the Network Device Enrollment Service and root CA certificate:

URL	Root CA certificate	
https://scep1.contoso.com/certsrv/mscep/ms...	C:\Users\mc_adm\Documents\AzureMgmtCe...	Add...
		Edit...
		Remove

In the preceding screenshot, you can see the configuration screen in the wizard to deploy the certificate enrollment point in Configuration Manager. For the URL, enter the address in the `https://<FQDN>/certsrv/mscep/mscep.dll` format. For the root certificate, you should browse for the certificate file of your certificate authority. If you are using certificates in Configuration Manager, this will be the same certificate that you imported in the **Client Communication** tab in **Site Settings**.

When this is configured on the server that runs the NDES, log on as a domain administrator and copy the files listed from the `<ConfigMgrInstallationMedia>\` `SMSSETUP\POLICYMODULE\X64` folder on the Configuration Manager installation media to a folder on your server:

- `PolicyModule.msi`
- `PolicyModuleSetup.exe`

On the **Certificate Registration Point** page, specify the URL of the certificate registration point and the virtual application name. The default virtual application name is `CMCertificateRegistration`. For example, if the site system server has an FQDN of `scep1.contoso.com` and you used the default virtual application name, specify `https://scep1.contoso.com/CMCertificateRegistration`.

Creating certificate profiles

Click on **Certificate Profiles** in the **Assets and Compliance** workspace under the **Compliance Settings** folder.

Specify general information about this certificate profile

Name: Corporate Wi-Fi Certificate

Description:

Specify the type of certificate profile that you want to create.

○ Trusted CA certificate

◉ Simple Certificate Enrollment Protocol (SCEP) settings

On the **General** page, provide the name and description of the profile, and then provide information about the type of certificate that you want to deploy. Select the **trusted CA certificate** profile type if you want to deploy a trusted root **certification authority (CA)** or intermediate CA certificate, for example, you might want to deploy you own internal CA certificate to your own workgroup devices managed by Configuration Manager.

Select the SCEP certificate profile type if you want to request a certificate for a user or device using the Simple Certificate Enrollment Protocol and the Network Device Enrollment Service role service.

You will be provided with different settings depending on the option that you specify. If you select **SCEP**, then you will be asked about the number of retries and storage information about TPM. You can find specific information about each of the settings on the TechNet library at `http://bit.ly/1n5CtZF`.

Configuring a trusted CA certificate is much simpler; provide the certificate settings and the destination store, as shown in the following screenshot:

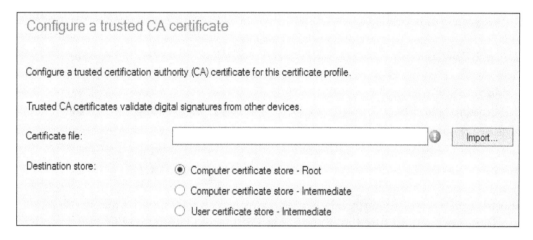

When you have finished configuring information on your certificate profile, select the supported platforms for the profile and continue through the wizard to create the profile. When it has been created, you can right-click on the profile to deploy it to a collection.

Managing VPN profiles with Configuration Manager

At a high level, the process to create VPN profiles is the same as creating Wi-Fi profiles; no prerequisites are required such as deploying certificates. Click on **VPN Profiles** in the **Assets and Compliance** workspace under the `Compliance Settings` folder. Create a new VPN profile, and on the initial screen, provide simple information about the profile.

The following table provides an overview of which profiles are supported on which device:

Connection type	iOS	Windows 8.1	Windows RT	Windows RT 8.1	Windows Phone 8.1
Cisco AnyConnect	Yes	No	No	No	No
Juniper Pulse	Yes	Yes	No	Yes	Yes
F5 Edge Client	Yes	Yes	No	Yes	Yes
Dell SonicWALL Mobile Connect	Yes	Yes	No	Yes	Yes
Check Point Mobile VPN	Yes	Yes	No	Yes	Yes
Microsoft SSL (SSTP)	No	Yes	Yes	Yes	No
Microsoft Automatic	No	Yes	Yes	Yes	No
IKEv2	No	Yes	Yes	Yes	Yes
PPTP	Yes	Yes	Yes	Yes	No
L2TP	Yes	Yes	Yes	Yes	No

Specific options will be required, depending on which technology you choose from the drop-down list. Ensure that the settings are specified and move on to the profile information in the authentication method.

Configure the authentication method to use for this VPN profile

Authentication method:

RSA SecurID

☐ Remember the user credentials at each logon

If you require proxy settings with your VPN profile, then specify these settings on the **Proxy Settings** page of the wizard. See the following screenshot for an example of this screen:

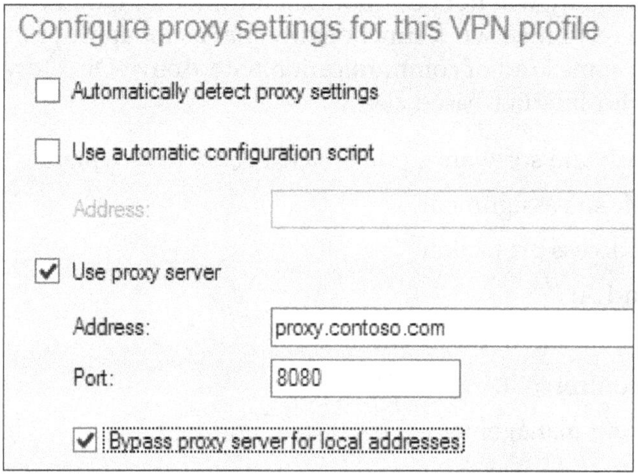

Configure proxy settings for this VPN profile

☐ Automatically detect proxy settings

☐ Use automatic configuration script

Address:

☑ Use proxy server

Address: proxy.contoso.com

Port: 8080

☑ Bypass proxy server for local addresses

Continue through the wizard and select the supported profiles for the profile. When the profile is created, you can right-click on the profile and select **Deploy**.

Managing Internet-based devices

We have already looked at deploying certain company resources to those clients to whom we have very little connectivity on a regular basis. We can use Configuration Manager to manage these devices just like those domain-based clients over the Internet.

This scenario works really well when the clients do not use VPN or DirectAccess, or maybe when we do not deploy a remote access solution for our remote users. This is where we can use Configuration Manager to manage clients using **Internet-based client management (IBCM)**.

How Internet-based client management works

We have the ability to manage Internet-based clients in Configuration Manager by deploying certain site system roles in DMZ. By doing this, we make the management point, distribution point, and software update point Internet-facing and configure clients to connect to this while on the Internet.

With these measures in place, we now have the ability to manage clients that are on the Internet, extending our management capabilities.

Functionality in Internet-based client management

In general, functionality will not be supported for Internet-based client management when we have to rely on network functionality that is not appropriate on a public network or relies some kind of communication with Active Directory. The following is not supported for Internet-based clients:

- Client push and software-update-based client deployment
- Automatic site assignment
- Network access protection
- Wake-On-LAN
- Operating system deployment
- Remote control
- Out-of-band management

 Software distribution for users is only supported when the Internet-based management point can authenticate the user in Active Directory using the Windows authentication.

Requirements for Internet-based client management

In terms of requirements, the list is fairly short but depending on your current setup, this might take a while to set up. The first seems fairly obvious, but any site system server or client must have Internet connectivity. This might mean some firewall configuration, depending on your configuration.

A **public key infrastructure** (**PKI**) is also required. It must be able to deploy and manage certificates to clients that are on the Internet and site systems that are Internet-based. This does not mean deploying certificates over the public Internet.

The following information can help you plan and deploy Internet-based client management in your environment:

- Planning for Internet-based client management (http://bit.ly/1p1qtsU)
- Planning for certificates (http://bit.ly/1kj9PFr)
- PKI certificate requirements (http://bit.ly/1hssMFM)

Using Internet-based client management

As the administrator, you have no additional concerns and requirements in terms of how you manage your clients when they are based on the Internet and are reporting to an Internet-facing management point.

When you are administering clients that are Internet-based, you will see them report to the Internet-facing management point. This is the only thing you will see. You will see that the preceding features we listed are not working.

The icon for the client in the list of devices does not change; this is one of the reasons the functionality is powerful, as it gives you many of the management capabilities you already perform on your premise devices.

Lots of people will implement DirectAccess to get around the need to set up additional Configuration Manager Infrastructure and provisioning certificates. DirectAccess with the Manage Out functionality is a viable alternative.

Using the Microsoft Exchange connector

Configuration Manager provides you with the ability to use the abilities of ActiveSync to collect a basic inventory on cell phones and provides limited management options. Different devices have different capabilities but can be broken down into two roles as follows:

- **The mobile device legacy client management**: These devices will have the mobile device legacy client deployed to them in order to manage devices for inventory as well as to configure corporate policies using settings management and software distribution. This functionality requires the use of a PKI environment and a management point and distribution point.
- **Exchange Server connector**: We can use the Exchange Server connector to perform basic management such as the collection of inventory and management of policies using ActiveSync.

This process works by establishing a data feed between Configuration Manager and the Exchange Server. From here, data is extracted from the mobile device and loaded into the Configuration Manager database as a discovery record.

The configuration of the connector is simple; all that is required is a service account or the computer account of the primary site and the appropriate permissions to Exchange as well as the Exchange Server name. To achieve this, we use a service account that has necessary rights to an Exchange Server in order to discover basic management information from devices connected to it.

The level of access at Exchange will define the features that are available. For example, write access on Exchange is required to set mobile policies or wipe the device through Exchange. As the name indicates, a wipe will reset the phone in case it is lost or stolen. If the administrator chooses, this can be done from Configuration Manager Console.

Connecting to Exchange using the connector

Configuration Manager 2012 has a built-in wizard for the Exchange Connector, which allows us to easily set up the connection to the Exchange Server for discovery. The wizard also provides settings for discovery frequency and policies to manage.

The connector has the ability to connect to both on-premise Exchange environments and those that are part of an Office 365 subscription. From within the **Administration** workspace, expand **Hierarchy Configuration** and click on **Exchange Server Connectors**.

Create a new connector and you will see the following screenshot where you can select between an on-premise Exchange and a hosted Exchange environment:

In the preceding screenshot, our example is pointing to the hosted Exchange option, which is an Office 365 subscription. Just like the on-premise option, you must use an account with the appropriate permissions. The following screenshot shows you the permissions required. These are the same for both server options.

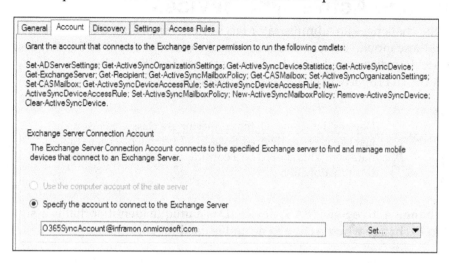

In the **Settings** tab, you can define any settings you wish to configure, as you can see in the following screenshot that shows you the settings available for password management:

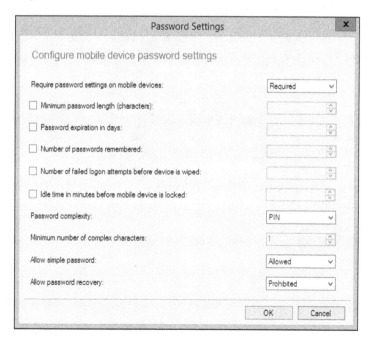

When you have configured the connector, it will run once, then on the schedule that you have defined in the **Connectors Settings**.

Managing ActiveSync devices

One of the challenges an administrator faces after onboarding this service is to separate these mobile devices from bloating the machine count in the database. Mobile devices discovered from Exchange can be identified using the `EAS_DeviceID` property from the system resource.

 Devices that come via the connector are classes as resources just like users or devices. So, add additional objects to the database. This should be a consideration before implementing this functionality.

The **Exchange Active Sync (EAS)** device ID is a unique identifier that is assigned and stored in **Exchange when Active Sync** and is used for connection.

Here is a screenshot of the example criteria that we can use to filter out devices that are in the database via the connector. This is added to a new query-based collection membership rule.

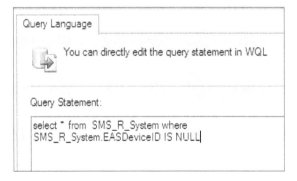

This is a simple way to make sure your collections are nice and clean and your report accuracy is maintained as well.

Using Windows Intune

Windows Intune is a cloud-based technology from Microsoft that enables you to manage Windows, iOS, and Android-based devices. Like Office 365, Windows Intune is a subscription-based service and prices are based on a per-user model.

You can also configure Windows Intune to connect to Configuration Manager. This is known as **Unified Device Management (UDM)**.

When UDM is in use, you are able to protect company data while letting users enroll their mobile devices and giving them access to the company data.

Requirements for Windows Intune

Before you can begin your integration with Configuration Manager, a number of requirements are needed; these are both external to Configuration Manager as well as a connector within Configuration Manager.

You must have a public-verifiable domain name that can be verified in the Windows Intune administration portal. Your user accounts must also have valid UPN entries for the public domain in your organization.

Directory synchronization is also required. A number of methods are available for performing this task. Check the TechNet documentation at `http://bit.ly/1pMMWtj` for a detailed explanation on the methods available to you.

Depending on the devices you wish to manage, a number of certificates might be required. You can also find more information about the certificates that are required on TechNet at `http://bit.ly/1hS2YgA`.

Deploying the Windows Intune connector

The connector for Configuration Manager allows you to specify your Windows Intune subscription settings for the service. You must specify a collection, which will determine the users that are allowed to enroll their devices and which mobile platforms you wish to support.

 When the Windows Intune subscription has been created, you can deploy the Windows Intune connector site system role to connect to the Windows Intune service.

The connector is responsible for pushing settings and applications to the Windows Intune service and will also act as the point to receive inventory from Windows Intune. The following operations are performed during the initial configuration:

- Retrieving the certificate that the Windows Intune connector requires to connect to the Windows Intune service
- Defining the user collection that enables users to enroll mobile devices
- Defining and configuring the mobile platforms that you want to support and setting the company logo

Creating the subscription within Configuration Manager is a simple process. In your console, navigate to the **Administration** workspace. From here, if you are using Service Pack 1, then expand **Hierarchy Configuration**, and then click on the **Windows Intune Subscriptions** node. If you are using R2, then expand cloud services and click on **Windows Intune Subscriptions**.

Next, depending on your version of Configuration Manager, click on either **Create Windows Intune Subscription** or **Add Windows Intune Subscription**. Then, proceed through the wizard and sign in to your Windows Intune subscription. Select the **Allow the Configuration Manager console to manage this subscription** checkbox.

In the **General** tab, specify a collection that contains users who are allowed to enroll their devices through Windows Intune. You can also specify your company name and the URL to your company's privacy policy documentation.

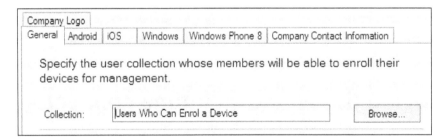

 If a user is removed from the collection, the user's device will continue to be managed for up to 24 hours till the user record is removed from the user database.

When these settings have been configured, you will need to deploy the connector to either a new site server or an existing site server. On the **System Role Selection** page, select **Windows Intune Connector** and continue through the wizard.

Enrolling mobile devices with Windows Intune

Using the Windows Phone operating system, the enrollment of devices is done via **Settings** and then **Company Apps**. Here, enter your e-mail address and password and click on **Enroll**, as shown in the following screenshot:

If you are using an iOS device or an Android device, you must download the Company Portal application from the vendor's application store. Once this has been downloaded and installed, the process is similar to the preceding one.

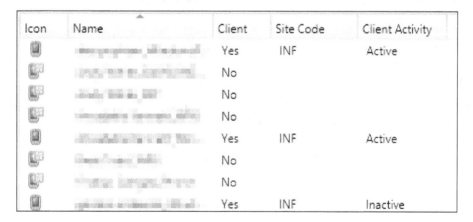

Icon	Name	Client	Site Code	Client Activity
		Yes	INF	Active
		No		
		No		
		No		
		Yes	INF	Active
		No		
		No		
		Yes	INF	Inactive

Unlike devices that are managed via the Internet, devices that are provisioned via Windows Intune will have a different icon. They will appear with a mobile phone icon in the list of devices; you can see this in the preceding screenshot:

 By default, devices are assigned the ownership status of **Personal**. You can change them in the console using PowerShell.

Devices that are personal will only have inventory collected for applications that are installed by Configuration Manager. You can use the ownership status in a global condition for application deployment as well, if you need to.

Although the icon is different, these devices can be managed in the same way as other resources in your Configuration Manager environment. You can create collections from these devices as well as deploy applications to them, and deploy compliance baselines, settings, as well as resource profiles.

Summary

In this chapter, we explored a number of ways in which you can manage the growing popularity of bring your own device and also look at how we can manage mobility in your user estate.

We explored the deployment of profiles that contain settings for Wi-Fi profiles, VPN profiles for Windows, and other devices as well as deploying certificates via Configuration Manager.

We also looked at using Configuration Manager to configure integration with Exchange both on premise and through Office 365 as well as how to configure Windows Intune for unified device management.

In the next chapter, we will look at how to troubleshoot your Configuration Manager environment. We will explore the many logfiles that are available in Configuration Manager as well as look at some Microsoft and community tools that are available to help you troubleshoot your environment.

12
Advanced Troubleshooting

Now that you have designed and implemented your environment, the biggest challenge you will face is the maintenance of the environment and troubleshooting when things go wrong. In general, Configuration Manager will not manage by itself; it often requires your administrative input. As part of this process, you will need to learn how to troubleshoot your environment when things go wrong.

Anyone who is familiar with Configuration Manager will already know that the logging capabilities are immense. Any error you need to find will almost certainly be found in one of the numerous logfiles. A number of tools are available from both Microsoft and third parties to help with the diagnostic and troubleshooting process. In this chapter, we will look at the troubleshooting process and the use of free tools and help you troubleshoot your environment:

- How to trace errors using logfiles
- Using toolkit resources for troubleshooting
- Using the service manager utility
- Real-world troubleshooting scenarios

Error tracing in Configuration Manager

By default, logging is enabled within Configuration Manager for client and server components. Each individual component has its own logfile, which you will need for troubleshooting that component.

Most of the processes within Configuration Manager log operational information to logfiles. These files can be identified by the usual extension for a logfile, which is .LOG. When this logfile is full, the file is copied to a file with the same name but with the extension .LO_. When the master logfile is full again, the contents of the file with the .LO_ extension are overwritten and the process is repeated.

Sometimes, depending on the problem that you are trying to troubleshoot, you might need to look in multiple logfiles to troubleshoot a specific process or just to trace the problem back to where it was originally triggered.

To view logfiles, you can use the Configuration Manager log viewer tool called CMTrace. By default, this is located in the SMSSETUP\TOOLS folder of the setup media and can also be found in the tools folder where you installed Configuration Manager.

To view logfiles during the operating system deployment, CMTrace is also added to the boot images, which are added to **Software Library**.

Modifying the logging options for components

You can use Configuration Manager Service Manager, which is discussed later in this chapter, to restart services in Configuration Manager in order to also modify the logging options for a specific component.

When you open Service Manager from the Monitoring workspace and the **Component Status** node from the ribbon, right-click on a component in the list. From the context menu that appears, click on **Logginvg**.

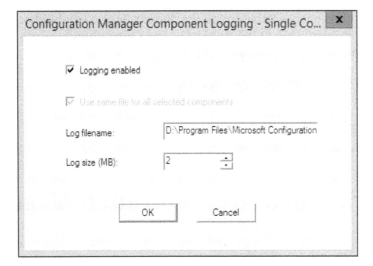

The options that are available to you are basic, but if required, you can turn off logging for a specific component as well as change the location of the logfile and the size of the log. The size that is entered is the size at which the logfile will rotate and a new log will be started.

 Generally, it is not required to change the properties from the default settings for each component; however, this provides you with flexibility, should you need it.

If you require verbose logging on any component on the site server, then you can use the registry editor to enable more verbose logging. In the registry editor, navigate to the HKLM\SOFTWARE\Microsoft\SMS\COMPONENTS key.

From here, you can select the component to which you wish to enable additional verbose logging. When you have selected the component, you need the **Verbose Logging DWORD** value to be changed to one of the following:

Value	Meaning
0	Error and key messages; this is the default value
1	Everything mentioned previously as well as additional information
2	Verbose; this is the highest logging level

When you have completed the changes you need, restart the SMS Executive service, and then open the appropriate log. You will see more information entering the logfile than usual.

Where to find specific logfiles

By default, Configuration Manager logfiles are stored in a variety of locations that depend on the process that creates the logfile and on the configuration of your site systems. Because the location of the log on a given computer can vary, use search to locate the relevant logfiles on your Configuration Manager computers in order to help you troubleshoot a specific scenario.

You can find a list of all the logfiles available in Configuration Manager as well as a list of all the logfiles for specific components in the TechNet documentation at http://bit.ly/1qG3i9j.

Using the Configuration Manager toolkit

The Configuration Manager toolkit is a free set of tools available from Microsoft that assists with the management and diagnosis of issues on your Configuration Manager site. The toolkit can be downloaded from the Microsoft website and is frequently updated at `http://bit.ly/1m8qfAB`.

The tools available are split up in two categories: server- and client-based tools. We will look at both categories here.

Using server-based diagnostic tools

A number of tools are available in the server-based tools package in order to help diagnose and troubleshoot issues with your Configuration Manager site. The following tools are available in this package:

- DP Job Manager
- Collection Evaluation Viewer
- Content Library Explorer
- Security Configuration Wizard
- Content Library Transfer
- Content Ownership Tool
- Role-based Administration Modeling and Auditing Tool
- Run Meter Summarization Tool

We will look at the following four tools from this package in more detail:

- DP Job Manager
- Collection Evaluation Viewer
- Content Library Explorer
- Content Ownership Tool

While the other tools will help with the management of your environment, they are unlikely to provide any value in troubleshooting issues in your environment.

Using the DP job manager tool

If you have installed the toolkit to the default directory, you will find the DP job manager in the `ServerTools` directory within `C:\Program Files (x86)\ConfigMgr 2012 Toolkit R2`, which is the default directory. Here, the tool can be launched by double-clicking on `DPJobMgr.exe`. Make sure that you run the tool with the correct account that has permissions within Configuration Manager.

When the tool launches, enter the name of your primary site and click on **Connect**. This will then connect to the primary site; you can see the tool connecting in the bottom-left corner of the window. Once the tool is connected, you will see the text as shown in the following screenshot:

Connect to Site Server ▄▅▆▆▋▋ was successful!

Once you see the tool connected, you are ready to proceed and use the tool. In the **Overview** tab, you will see the tool list out the distribution points in your environment. You will also see a count of jobs and running jobs in your environment. This is useful if you are having problems with packages going down to distribution points.

		Total Distribution Points	1
Total Running Jobs	0	Total Jobs	1

Running Jobs	Total Jobs	Total Retries
0	1	0

You can also see a count of jobs that are queued up and running per distribution point. Again, this will get highlighted if you have a problem with a specific distribution point or the distribution manager.

In the distribution point information tab, you will see some really useful information per distribution point. Here, you will see what is getting distributed to your distribution points at a content level. You will also see the size of the package as well as the start time and more importantly, the progress of the package distribution and the number of retries.

		Total Distribution Points	1
Total Distribution Points Selected	1	Total Jobs	1

Progress %	Start/Restart Time	Retries	Distribution Point Name
	14/08/2014 17:20:38		MCUKCM02.MCUK....

The **Manage Jobs** tab will show you the same information as the distribution point information tab but will give you a context menu where you can control the job and force a retry of the content distribution.

 The DP job manager tool is really useful for diagnosing problems with content that is stuck or is not getting distributed to distribution points properly.

Using the collection evaluation viewer tool

The collection evaluation viewer tool can be found in the **ServerTools** directory of the toolkit installation; you can launch it by double-clicking on the CEViewer.exe executable. The tool should be run on the site server rather than a remote machine; the only permissions you need to use this tool are the read-only analyst role and db_datareader on the site database in SQL.

This tool will be used to investigate issues with collection membership. It is quite common where query rules are concerned that they are not written properly, which can cause numerous problems with the collection evaluation.

There are four threads that run in order to evaluate the collections in the preceding queues. Each queue includes a series of arrays, and each array includes the collections to be evaluated. The thread that is running for the queue selects a collection from the array and runs the evaluation. The queue length indicates the number of arrays in the queue.

The four threads or queues that you can view in the tool are as follows:

- **Manual Queue**: This is for collections that are manually selected for evaluation using the administration console
- **New Queue**: This is for collections that are newly created; it is always a full update in reality as the collection has just been created
- **Full Queue**: This is for collections that are due for full evaluation as per the schedule setting on the collection
- **Incremental Queue**: This is for collections that are due for a delta or incremental evaluation, for example, new resources are added

Connect to the primary site, as with the DP job manager, the connection status is shown in the bottom-left corner of the screen. The **Full Evaluation** tab will provide you with a grid of all your collections and show you some detailed information about the evaluation process.

If you run this process on a remote computer, you will most likely need the SQL Server certificate importing, just as we did in the reporting chapter.

As you can see in the following screenshot, we can see that our **All Systems** collection had a total runtime of **3.7970** seconds and had zero membership changes. We can also see that **All Users and User Groups** had a runtime of **2.3590** seconds.

Connect	Full Evaluation	Incremental Evaluation	All Queues	Manual Queue	New Queue	Full Queue	Incremental Queue	About Collection Evaluation		

Refresh	Start Auto Refresh	Auto Refresh Interval (minutes)	5			Total Run Time	00:00:20	Total Collections	15
		Site Code	MUK	Full Evaluation					

Collection Name	Site ID	Run Time (seconds)	Last Evaluation Completion Time	Next Evaluation Time	Member Changes	Last Member Change Time	Percent
All Systems	SMS00001	3.7970	14/08/2014 17:09:32	15/08/2014 04:00:00	0	07/02/2014 12:36:37	18.398
All Users and User Groups	SMS00004	2.3590	14/08/2014 17:09:41	15/08/2014 04:00:00	0	05/08/2014 11:56:16	11.430

We can also see the total runtime for all of the collections that run through the full evaluation process at the top-right corner of this tab. This tab is very useful to see whether some collections are taking a long time to process; this could be taking up resources on the database and the primary site.

The incremental evaluation tab shows up the same information but based on the previous incremental evaluation schedule that was run. All queues will show us the queue status of the queues that we have previously mentioned. In the following screenshot, we triggered a manual console update of **All Systems**, which means that any collection that is built on this one will also be updated as part of this process. Processing improvements means that if you update a parent collection, only the children are updated. This can reduce the processing time required, but it can still be quite high. We can see in the following screenshot that this is part of one job, as the queue length for all 35 collections is set to one:

Summary		
	Coll. #	Q. Len.
Manual Update	11	1
New Collection		
Full Evaluation		
Inc Evaluation		
Total	11	1

Running Evaluations	
Started on	Elapsed (seconds)
Manual Update	
All Systems	
08/14 05:27:39 PM	1.352

You can use the other four tabs for each of the queues in order to look at them in more detail. This can be useful for looking at specific collection update issues, seeing how many new members have been discovered, and how long the evaluation process is taking.

Using the content library explorer tool

The content library explorer is a tool that will help with troubleshooting issues with the content library. As we have already discovered in a previous chapter, the way Configuration Manager stores content is different from previous versions of Configuration Manager, so this tool exists in order to help us troubleshoot issues in this area.

The following screenshot of the data library inside the content library shows you how the structure looks. This is why using this tool is critical to browse the library easily.

The tool can be launched from the **ServerTools** directory in the installation path for the toolkit and can be loaded by double-clicking on `ContentLibraryExplorer.exe`.

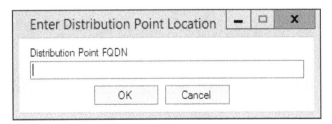

Enter the fully qualified domain name of a distribution point that you want to explore. This tool connects to a single distribution point. When the tool has connected the tree on the left-hand side of the window, you should see the contents listed.

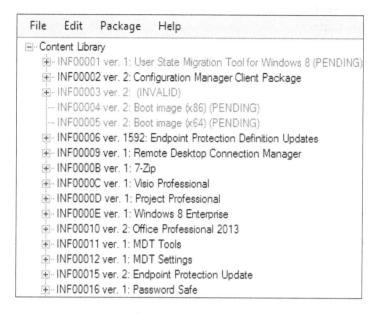

When you click on a package on the left-hand side, the right pane is populated with information about the package, including the filename of specific files, the size, and the drive on which the file is locally located on the distribution point. This is shown due to the single instance storage and the fact that the content library can span multiple drives and the content might be on a different drive.

On the right-hand side of the window, you will find the full path to the file on the content library in the share format. This tool can be incredibly helpful to manually validate packages if you need to, initiating a redistribution of the content. This can all be done from the **Package** menu.

Using the content ownership tool

As with the previous tools, you can launch the content ownership tool by double-clicking on `ContentOwnershipTool.exe` from the **ServerTools** directory of the toolkit installation path.

This tool will automatically connect to your site, so it needs to be run locally on the site server rather than a remote machine. By default, the tool will only show orphaned packages that effectively have no site owner. This can happen post migration but can happen due to problems with the site or after a site failure.

The content ownership tool allows you to assign content to a specific site; the tool will show you information about the package. Simply tick the packages you wish to act upon, and then, from the bottom of the screen, select the site that you wish to transfer the ownership to and click on **Apply**. You can view the logfile of this process by clicking on **View Log** on the far right-hand side, as shown in the following screenshot:

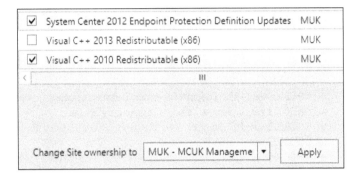

From experience, I can say that it is rare that this tool is needed; however, when you do come across content ownership issues, it can save you lots of time, so it is a very valid tool in your arsenal.

Using client-based diagnostic tools

As with the server-based tools, a number of client-based tools are also available to help with diagnosis and troubleshooting. The tools that are available in this package are as follows:

- Client Spy
- Trace Log Viewer
- The Deployment Monitoring tool
- Policy Spy
- The Power Viewer tool
- The Send Schedule tool
- Wakeup Spy

In this chapter, we will look at the use of the Client Spy, Policy Spy, and the Deployment Monitoring tool.

Using the Client Spy tool

Client Spy helps you troubleshoot issues related to software distribution, inventory, and software metering on Configuration Manager clients. Client Spy can be launched by double-clicking on CliSpy.exe from the **ClientTools** directory of the toolkit installation.

The tool allows for remote or local execution. In order to connect to a remote machine, select **Tools and Connect**. By default, the tool will bind locally to the client, if one exists. Three options are available on the tools menu; these are **Software Distribution, Inventory**, and **Software Metering**.

Firstly, on software distribution, you will see any pending execution requests that are outstanding on the client. We can also see the execution history as well as cache information and information on any pending executions.

The inventory option will provide us with high-level information on when the last inventory cycle for each client was as well as information on the data discovery record or DDR.

As you can see from the preceding screenshot, we are looking at information on the DDR for this client. We can see the version information as well as the date of the last report and when the last cycle started.

If we expand instances, we can also see information on what was collected. Expand an instance key further, and you will see information telling us whether this specific key was collected with a true or false value or not and the value that was returned.

Using the Policy Spy tool

Policy Spy can be launched by double-clicking on the PolicySpy.exe executable from the **ClientTools** directory of the toolkit installation.

This tool is great for the troubleshooting policy on your clients in Configuration Manager; it must be launched as an administrator as well. One of the features of Policy Spy is the ability to export a policy to an XML file. In the **Tools** menu, we have a number of options, as shown in the following screenshot:

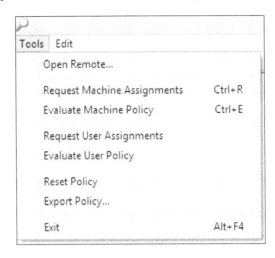

Let's have a look at these features in a little more detail:

- **Request Machine Assignments**: This option is if you want to trigger a machine policy refresh. When this has been triggered, you can monitor the `PolicyAgent.log` logfile for more details on the request and reply from the management point.

- **Evaluate Machine Policy**: This option triggers a machine policy evaluation; the troubleshooting information can then be found in the `PolicyEvaluator.log` file on the client.

- **Request User Assignments**: This option will trigger a refresh of the user policy for the currently logged-on user and not the user running the tool. The troubleshooting information can be found in the `PolicyAgent.log` file.

- **Evaluate User Policy**: This option will trigger a user policy evaluation; the troubleshooting information can be found in the `PolicyEvaluator.log` file.

- **Reset Policy**: This option will remove all of the non-default policies from the client and then trigger a machine policy request.

- **Export Policy**: This option will allow you to export the policy in an XML format for further analysis and troubleshooting.

The default schedule for all of the policy assignments is 60 minutes; this is when the client will attempt to refresh its policy. This can be configured in the client settings in the administration console.

A number of tabs are available within Policy Spy as well, and these tabs are as follows:

- **Actual**
- **Requested**
- **Default**
- **Events**

The **Actual** tab shows us which policies are actually applied on the client, both for the computer and the user. The results are displayed in a tree format with the top node for the machine, and then, each subsequent node is a user-specific namespace, as shown in the following screenshot:

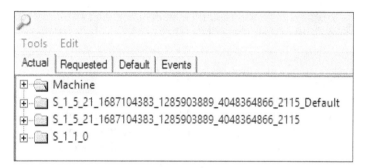

When we expand the **Machine** node, you will see a number of classes, such as CCM_ClientActions. These relate to other actions, such as hardware inventory, software inventory, and discovery inventory.

On the **Requested** tab, you will see policy assignments that were retrieved from the client's assigned site. Results are displayed in a tree format, as with the **Actual** tab. This allows you to troubleshoot differences in the policies between the **Actual** and **Requested** tabs. A difference might indicate a problem with the client who is processing the policy, or it might indicate an issue-requesting policy from the management point.

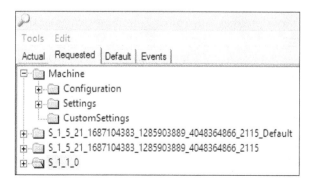

When you expand the **Machine** node, as shown in the preceding screenshot, you will see the **Configuration** and **Settings** node. Here is a short explanation of what each node shows:

- **Configuration**: This displays a list of configuration classes that are derived from CCM_Policy_Config. This includes policy objects, assignments, and other settings.

- **Settings**: This node displays all the active settings that are generated by the policies. The settings' values are displayed under the **Configuration** node.

Multiple instances can exist with the same names because these settings have not been merged into a final policy. Policy Spy displays instances under this node using the RealKey property instead of their true policy. They can be easily correlated to the merged policy displayed on the **Actual** tab.

The **Events** tab displays policy events as they happen on the client. The view creates an event subscription for all events from the CCM_PolicyAgent_Event class. The view shows a maximum of 200 events and then removes the oldest events from the list. If the last item in the list is selected, Policy Spy will automatically scroll down when new events are added. Otherwise, the view maintains its current position at all times, and you must manually scroll down or press the *End* key to view new events. This view will always be empty when viewing an exported policy in Policy Spy.

Using the deployment monitoring tool

The deployment monitoring tool is launched from the **ClientTools** directory in the toolkit installation by double-clicking on DeploymentMonitoringTool.exe. The tool is a graphical interface that is designed to help troubleshoot application, update, and baseline deployments.

This tool can be executed locally on a client, or you can connect to a remote client. From the **Actions** menu, you can perform a number of actions. They are as follows:

- Connect to a remote machine for remote diagnostics of the deployments on a specific client

- Import and export XML files from another system for further troubleshooting and analysis

- View the logfile depending on which option is selected; this will be either the PolicyAgent.log, UpdatesDeployment.log, or the WindowsUpdate.log file on the client

The **Client Properties** tab will help us get all the client details. The information on **Monitor Host**, **Monitor Running As**, **Monitor Connected To**, **Client OS**, and **OS Version** is very helpful at the time of troubleshooting, as shown in the following screenshot:

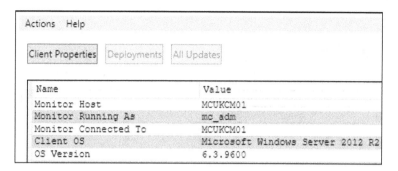

The **Deployments** tab will help you list the details of each targeted deployment. This will provide you with details, such as **Name**, **Deadline**, **Status**, **Type**, and **ID** of the deployment, as shown in the following screenshot:

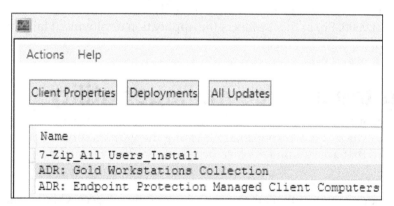

When you click on a specific deployment such as the one named 7-Zip_All Users_Install, as shown in the preceding screenshot, you will get more details at the bottom of the screen. A number of tabs are available at the bottom of the screen when selecting a deployment, which provides you with more detailed information about the deployment.

Using applications in Configuration Manager, you can add requirements to a deployment type. You can review the evaluation of these requirements using the requirement violations tab. You will be able to see the current value that has been evaluated, the expression in a textual format, and the name of the rule.

CurrentValue	RuleExpression
AMD64	Equals AMD64
6.3.9600	BeginsWith 6.1
1	Equals 1
Microsoft Windows 8.1 Enterprise	NotEquals not_a_valid_os_caption
18	Equals 18

As you can see from the preceding screenshot, the evaluation for the installation of our application deployment has failed due to the highlighted condition. In this case, we can see that we were expecting an operating system version that begins with 6.1; however, this client is Windows 8.1 Update 1, which means that the version number is 6.3.9600. So, in this instance, the application deployment failed because the requirements were not met.

Using the service manager utility

The service manager tool is a part of the console. This tool does not require additional download. It is responsible for listing the various services and threads of those services that are running on specific servers in your hierarchy.

The tool enables you to view specific components that are either running or stopped and allows you to start, stop, and restart these specific services. Configuration Manager runs a number of processes off a single service, which is known as threads. Without the service manager, restarting a single service such as SMS_EXECUTIVE will result in the restart of lots of different threads within one service.

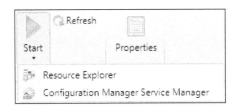

The service manager allows you to control the restarts of individual threads. This can be useful for troubleshooting and is commonly used when you want to force a component to attempt a reinstallation after it has failed.

Determining when to use the utility

In effect, the utility prevents the need for needlessly restarting the full environment by restarting SMS_EXECUTIVE. Depending on the issue that you are troubleshooting, this could potentially cause more problems. This is why the utility provides you with the ability to see the status of individual components rather than the overall service.

 While the service manager utility can be very useful for restarting components rather than the full services, use it only when you need to.

Configuration Manager is a schedule-based system and lots of tasks run only on a schedule that is not in demand.

An example of this is the site component manager that runs every 60 minutes. Another example of this is the distribution manager that is used to distribute content.

Many more examples of this exist in Configuration Manager. Some actions can be run again in the console but many of them cannot. In this instance, restarting the appropriate thread in the service manager will allow the queued tasks to be retried, thus avoiding the wait between attempts.

Restarting Configuration Manager services

Restarting components via the service manager utility is simple. You can launch the utility from the **Monitoring** workspace within the System Status folder, and you will see the **Component Status** node.

On the ribbon, click on **Start** and you will see **Configuration Manager Service Manager**. Click on this option to start the utility.

Real-world scenarios

In this section of the chapter, we will be looking at some common troubleshooting scenarios and using all the methods that we have learned to help us diagnose and debug the errors.

Troubleshooting content distribution errors

In order to troubleshoot content distribution errors, a number of logfiles exist, and tools might be required in order to determine where the problem is. For example, if you are having issues distributing content, then you will need to look at a number of logfiles and also use the DP job manager tool from the toolkit.

If we are having problems with content management on a cloud distribution point in Windows Azure, then we will need to look at a log on the site server called CloudDP-<guid>.log and replace the GUID with the unique identifier of the cloud distribution point. This log will contain information about storage and content access in the cloud-based distribution point. Additionally, CloudMgr.log will record and collect storage and bandwidth statistics as well as any actions in the console, such as starting or stopping the cloud service.

The main log that will be needed to troubleshoot content distribution errors from the site server to the distribution point is distmgr.log. This logfile contains information on the creation of packages and the compression and replication of packages as well as updates to packages.

The actual transfer process is recorded in the PkgXferMgr.log file on the site server. This log is responsible for recording the actions of the transfer process from the site server to the distribution point.

For a visual record of the transfer process, you should look at using the DP job manager tool, which was discussed earlier in this chapter. This tool will provide you with the troubleshooting information you need from a monitoring perspective and will find out whether the job has failed.

 You will still need to look at logfiles to determine the root cause of the problem.

Some of the most common errors that you will see with content distribution are as follows:

- Errors that occur when the site tries to take a snapshot of the content; you might see access denied or not found errors on the package source path

- If the remote distribution point is unavailable, then this will obviously cause you issues; you will see connectivity problems highlighted in the distribution manager logfile:

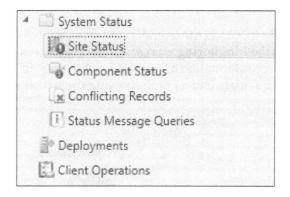

Don't forget, you can also use the **Monitoring** workspace to monitor the site and view summary messages. If you need more detail, though, then you really need to dig in to the logfiles.

Troubleshooting deployment errors

It is common to confuse the processes involved in the deployment process; you will hear people say they cannot deploy software to clients when, in fact, the issue lies with content distribution or failed deployments.

The most common issue with deployments comes down to the configuration of the deployment. Most of the things you will see are unexpected behavior. Configuration Manager will do what is asked of it, so it would not be common to see a problem with deployments caused by a fault in Configuration Manager.

You will possibly see issues related to deployments in Configuration Manager when the client is not processing the policy properly, requirements have not been evaluated properly, or the target machine is not in the correct collection.

You can use a combination of tools, such as Client Spy, Policy Spy, and the Deployment Monitoring tool on the client side to monitor this locally. You might also find use for the collection evaluation tool if the collection is not updating its membership properly.

Here, you can see a screenshot of the **Deployments** node in the console, showing you the list of deployments we have set up:

Software	Collection	Purpose	Action
7-Zip		Required	Install
7-Zip		Available	Install
7-Zip		Available	Install

You can use the console to look at the overall status of a deployment from the **Deployments** node in the **Monitoring** workspace. When you select an individual deployment, you will see information at the bottom of the screen, showing further information on the deployment and a graph showing the statistics of the deployment.

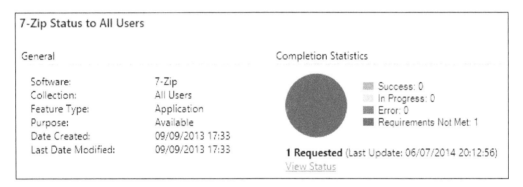

For the application deployment, you can use the AppIntentEval.log, AppDiscovery.log, and AppEnforce.log files locally on the client. These logfiles will record details about the current and intended state of applications, details about the discovery or detection of applications, and details on the enforcement actions taken for applications, respectively.

You can merge multiple logfiles from the trace log viewer. In the **Open** dialog, you will see the checkbox, as shown in the following screenshot:

Troubleshooting site system errors

Each of the components within Configuration Manager have their own logfile. Depending on the problem, you will have to look at the appropriate logfile. A number of logfiles exist for the management point and distribution point, for example, where some components only have a single logfile such as the distribution manager.

A list of the logfiles that are available in Configuration Manager for all the components and site systems can be found on TechNet at `http://bit.ly/1rRrJSX`. You can also use the **Component Status** node in the **Monitoring** workspace to view the health state of a component.

All components that are available over all of the servers in your hierarchy can be found in this section. If everything is working as it should, then a green tick will be displayed. Other states include a red cross for an error and a yellow triangle for a warning. The status change works on a summarization process. After a number of errors, which is a configurable value, the component will change its state.

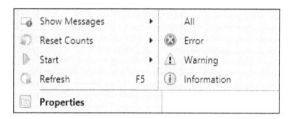

For each component, you can right-click and select the type of messages to be shown. You can also reset the counters, which will reset the state of the component, if required.

 Resetting the component status can be useful if you have resolved a problem and want to see the log reset in the console to determine whether the problem has been successfully resolved.

You can also view the thresholds that have been configured by right-clicking on a component and selecting **Properties**. You will see something similar to the following screenshot:

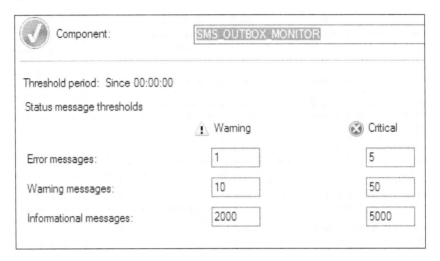

This information is useful if you want to see a summary of the number of messages that are required for the threshold to be breached. Here, it is important to make sure that you understand your environment so that you can tune the numbers, if required. This will stop needless errors.

Summary

In this chapter, we learned how to troubleshoot your Configuration Manager environment. We took a detailed look at the logfiles that are in Configuration Manager and looked at some of the more common logfiles you might need.

We also looked at how to use diagnostic tools as well as the service manager utility and some real-world troubleshooting examples.

I would like to finish off by saying that writing this book has been an amazing experience, and I hope you have enjoyed reading it as much as I have enjoyed writing it. Configuration Manager is all about knowledge; it is a massive product that has endless possibilities. If you can, set up a lab and try the steps in the book to improve your knowledge.

Index

Thank you for buying

Microsoft System Center Configuration Manager Advanced Deployment

About Packt Publishing

Packt, pronounced 'packed', published its first book "Mastering phpMyAdmin for Effective MySQL Management" in April 2004 and subsequently continued to specialize in publishing highly focused books on specific technologies and solutions.

Our books and publications share the experiences of your fellow IT professionals in adapting and customizing today's systems, applications, and frameworks. Our solution based books give you the knowledge and power to customize the software and technologies you're using to get the job done. Packt books are more specific and less general than the IT books you have seen in the past. Our unique business model allows us to bring you more focused information, giving you more of what you need to know, and less of what you don't.

Packt is a modern, yet unique publishing company, which focuses on producing quality, cutting-edge books for communities of developers, administrators, and newbies alike. For more information, please visit our website: www.packtpub.com.

About Packt Enterprise

In 2010, Packt launched two new brands, Packt Enterprise and Packt Open Source, in order to continue its focus on specialization. This book is part of the Packt Enterprise brand, home to books published on enterprise software – software created by major vendors, including (but not limited to) IBM, Microsoft and Oracle, often for use in other corporations. Its titles will offer information relevant to a range of users of this software, including administrators, developers, architects, and end users.

Writing for Packt

We welcome all inquiries from people who are interested in authoring. Book proposals should be sent to author@packtpub.com. If your book idea is still at an early stage and you would like to discuss it first before writing a formal book proposal, contact us; one of our commissioning editors will get in touch with you.

We're not just looking for published authors; if you have strong technical skills but no writing experience, our experienced editors can help you develop a writing career, or simply get some additional reward for your expertise.

Microsoft System Center 2012 Configuration Manager: Administration Cookbook

ISBN: 978-1-84968-494-1   Paperback: 224 pages

Over 50 practical recipes to administer System Center 2012 Configuration Manager

1. Administer System Center 2012 Configuration Manager.

2. Provides fast answers to questions commonly asked by new administrators.

3. Skip the why's and go straight to the how-to's.

4. Gain administration tips from System Center 2012 Configuration Manager MVPs with years of experience in large corporations.

Microsoft System Center Configuration Manager

ISBN: 978-1-78217-676-3   Paperback: 146 pages

Deploy a scalable solution by ensuring high availability and disaster recovery using Configuration Manager

1. Deploy highly available Configuration Manager sites and roles.

2. Back up, restore, and copy Configuration Manager to other sites.

3. Get to grips with performance tuning and best practices for Configuration Manager sites.

Please check **www.PacktPub.com** for information on our titles

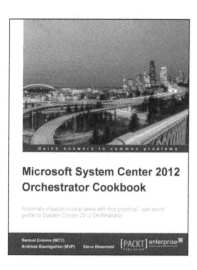

Microsoft System Center 2012 Orchestrator Cookbook

ISBN: 978-1-84968-850-5 Paperback: 318 pages

Automate mission-critical tasks with this practical, real-world guide to System Center 2012 Orchestrator

1. Create powerful runbooks for the System Center 2012 product line.

2. Master System Center 2012 Orchestrator by creating looping, child and branching runbooks.

3. Learn how to install System Center Orchestrator and make it secure and fault tolerant.

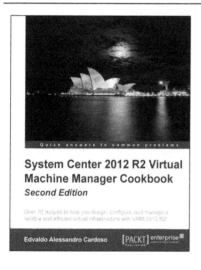

System Center 2012 R2 Virtual Machine Manager Cookbook

Second Edition

ISBN: 978-1-78217-684-8 Paperback: 428 pages

Over 70 recipes to help you design, configure, and manage a reliable and efficient virtual infrastructure with VMM 2012 R2

1. Create, deploy, and manage datacenters and private and hybrid clouds with hybrid hypervisors using VMM 2012 R2.

2. Integrate and manage fabric (compute, storages, gateways, and networking), services and resources, and deploy clusters from bare metal servers.

Please check **www.PacktPub.com** for information on our titles

www.ingramcontent.com/pod-product-compliance
Lightning Source LLC
Chambersburg PA
CBHW060521060326
40690CB00017B/3346